Inspired
Star Block Quilts

12 Projects Using Traditional and Modern Blocks

by Sandy Berg

Inspired
Star Block Quilts
by Sandy Berg

Landauer Publishing *(www.landauerpub.com)* is an imprint of
Fox Chapel Publishing Company, Inc.

Project Team:
Vice President–Content: Christopher Reggio
Editors: Laurel Albright/Sue Voegtlin
Copy Editor: Katie Ocasio
Designer: Laurel Albright
Photographer: Sue Voegtlin

ISBN: 978-1-947163-17-1

The Cataloging-in-Publication Data is on file with the Library of Congress.

We are always looking for talented authors. To submit an idea, please send a brief inquiry to
acquisitions@foxchapelpublishing.com.

Printed in China

21 20 19   2 4 6 8 10 9 7 5 3 1

Contents

Welcome to My World of Stars

Stars and quilts go together like so many other iconic duos. Stars have long played an important part in quilts because of their variety—they go from simple to very complex and everything in between. There are stars to suit every quilter's ability and purpose, from easy stars like a Variable Star or Friendship Star to the fancier versions like Lone Stars or Feathered stars. They are a universal image that needs no explanation. They pair easily with other blocks and design images and they can have different meanings to everyone.

They can represent everything from nature in a glorious night sky to patriotic feelings at the raising of a flag. Stars have long decorated quilts and they will continue to do so well into the future.

Sandy

Quilting Basics

Before we get going, I have some thoughts concerning tools and products used in quiltmaking. My best advice is to get to know the products you intend to use before using them in a project. Read the labels and test the products. This really applies to everything you will use in quiltmaking! Knowing what you are using and how to use it properly will give you much better results.

Quilting Terminology

As with many specialized areas, quilting has a lot of common terms and abbreviations. For your reference, here are some abbreviations that are used in these patterns.

- WOF = Width of Fabric—A cut of fabric that goes from one selvage to the selvage on the opposite side.

- RST = Right Sides Together—In sewing two pieces of fabric together, you place them with the right side of the fabrics facing one another.

- WST = Wrong Sides Together—In sewing two pieces of fabric together, you place them with the wrong side of the fabrics facing one another.

- HST = Half Square Triangle—This is a unit that is made from two triangles of fabric sewn together diagonally.

- QST = Quarter Square Triangle—This is a unit that is made from four 90° triangles of fabric sewn together diagonally.

- SS = Strip Set—This is the result of sewing two or more strips of fabric together. The strips are usually cut the width of the fabric (from selvage to selvage). After sewing these together, they are then cut apart in measured sections.

- WOF = width of fabric

- Sew with a ¼" (0.64cm) seam unless specified otherwise

Fabric Requirements and Preparation

Today's quilt fabrics are usually from 42" to 45" (1 to 1.15m) wide on the bolt. The patterns in this book assume 40" (1.02m) of usable fabric after removing the selvages, and the projects in this book are designed to use 100% cotton fabrics.

Before cutting pieces for your quilt, there are a few things I recommend doing.

- Remove the selvages from the fabric. This means taking off anywhere from ½" to ¾" (1.27 to 1.91cm) of fabric from the edges. Once you remove the selvages, you have a little less fabric to use for piecing.

- Pre-washing and protecting against color bleeding are not required, but it may save you heartache and disappointment later when/if you need to launder a completed project. Pre-washing, while not absolutely necessary, has it's advantages. Washing and drying your fabric will take care of any shrinkage and it will remove any excess dye that may remain in your fabric. Taking care of these two concerns at the beginning will alleviate the issues after you've completed your project and laundered it for the first time. No need to worry about color-fastness or shrinkage!

- An alternative to pre-washing your fabric is to test for color-fastness. It's a good idea when your fabric has a strong color, such as reds, deep purples, greens, or blues. Place a small piece of fabric in very hot water for about 15 minutes. If no color has bled into the water, you can consider it color-fast.

- If the color has transferred to the water, you know that this fabric will bleed when it gets wet. You can "set" the color in your fabric by using a laundry product that actually "catches" the color that may come out of your fabric. Quilt shops may carry a product used to set dyes, as well.

Batting

Whether you are new to quiltmaking or you are an experienced quilter, do your research on battings.

Wall hangings will probably never be washed. On the other hand, a quilt that will be used as a covering will need to be laundered at some point.

Batting comes in many different sizes and thickness, and different fiber content plays a huge roll in making a right choice for your project. Be sure to read the instructions on the batting to see if it is appropriate for the method of quilting you have chosen. On the label for the batting, you will find useful information such as how far apart the quilting should be, how much the batting will shrink when washed, and whether it is good for hand quilting or machine quilting.

There will be some shrinkage in the batting when you wash your project, so it will have a different appearance after washing. To see what your completed project may look like after it is washed, make up two quilted samples with your batting choice. Leave one unwashed, and machine wash and dry the other sample. Mark each test sample with the name of the batting, its fiber content, and whether it has been washed or not. Keep a collection of batting samples so you'll be able to choose the right batting for your future projects.

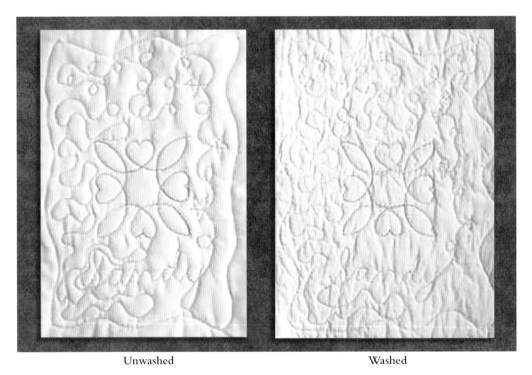

Unwashed   Washed

Here are a couple of batting samples; the unwashed one is on the left and the washed one is on the right. You can see the shrinkage between the two pieces and how much the quilting was "scrunched" up by washing and drying it.

Marking Tools, Rulers, and Templates

Marking tools, rulers, and templates . . . there are so many, all with different characteristics.

Always test your marking tools on small pieces of fabric from your project; they often act differently on different fabrics. You can determine how well you can see the marks and experiment with instructions for removal. In some markers, heat or detergents may permanently set the lines. Some come off in the washing process, some are easily removed with steam, and some, like a chalk marker, are simply brushed off. Follow the manufacturer's instructions for removal. If you are not able to completely remove the marks from your sample, select a different marker.

Templates are made by many manufacturers and usually perform very specific tasks. If you need a specific template for a project, ask your local quilt shop to recommend favorites. They are often willing to give you a demonstration on the use of a template. I used the Tri-Recs Tool™ Triangle Ruler by Darlene Zimmerman and Joy Hoffman to make star points. It's easy to use and gives you the option to make up to a 6½" (16.51cm) star point.

I created paper templates using this commercial template. You can make all star points with the templates beginning on page 108. I've also included a sashing strip template for the Star Crossing quilt on page 42. Use the instructions for making and using paper templates on page 8.

There is an abundance of rulers and templates available online and at your local fabric store. I suggest using the same brand for all your straight-edged rulers. That way, you know you will maintain accuracy when changing from one straight edge to another.

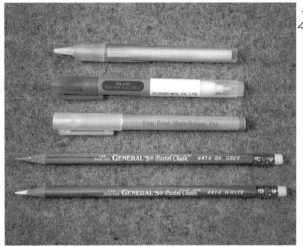

Marking Tools

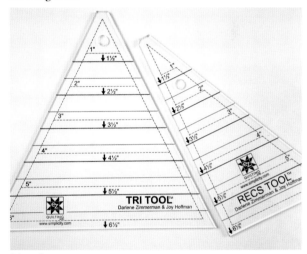

Templates

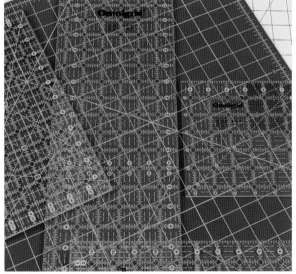

Use the same brand for all rulers

Shortcuts in Piecing

In quilt-making today, we are lucky because we have many shortcuts that can help make things faster and, sometimes, more accurate.

One of the shortcuts that I use frequently is the making of strip sets. Strip sets are strips of fabric that are cut from the width of fabrics, sewn together on the length of the strip, and then cut into smaller, usable segments. Sewing strip sets is faster and more accurate than cutting up smaller pieces, sewing them together, and pressing them. It minimizes the chance of the fabrics shifting as you start and stop sewing.

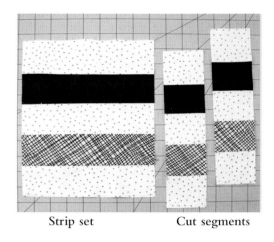

Strip set   Cut segments

To create a strip set, cut strips from the width of fabric. Sew the long strips together and press the seams open or to the darkest fabrics; whichever you prefer. Trim the selvages off the ends so that you have a straight edge to start cutting from. Cut off sections the width needed for the units you are making.

Strip sets are used in almost all of the patterns in the book, but there are many more shortcuts that can be used in other piecing techniques. If you are uncertain about a technique or looking for a shortcut, you can easily find many useful "how-to" videos on different topics on quilt shop websites and sites like YouTube. The best part is that you can view these as many times as needed until you are comfortable with the technique.

Making Elongated Star Points

This example shows the use of the Templates A and B from the Starry Night pattern, page 70, and Templates 1 and 2 for the stars in Star Chain, page 36. They work the same way but are a different size.

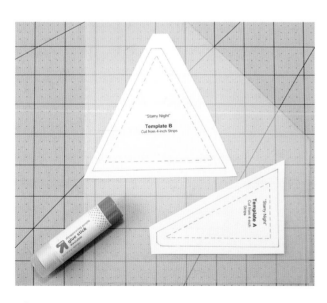

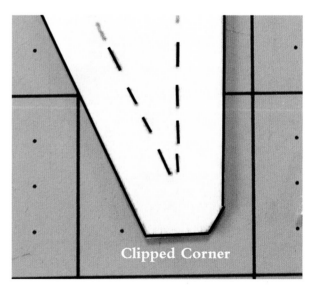

Clipped Corner

1   Cut outside of the solid lines of the paper templates, and then use a glue stick to adhere them to pieces of template plastic. Cut through both layers (paper and plastic), clipping off the small corner near the narrow end of the template. This is very important when aligning pieces within a project.

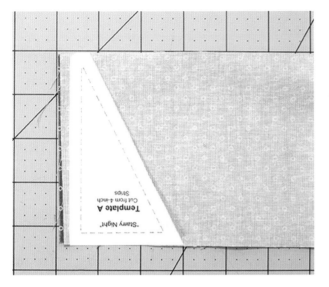

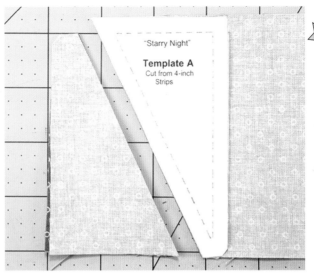

2 Two layers of fabric placed right sides together (RST) are used to cut the fabric for a star point. For this step-by-step, align the bottom of Template A with the bottom of the fabric strips. Cut out one template shape to make a left- and right-side star point. The star points will be mirror images of one another.

3 Rotate Template A, placing the template bottom on the top of the fabric strip, and cut another shape. Continue rotating the template and cut out the shapes. By cutting with the two strips RST, you will always end up with one shape that is the reverse of the other.

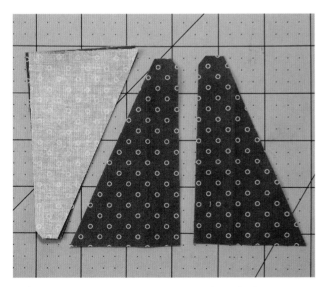

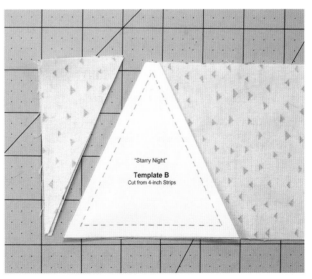

4 Keep the (2) shapes separated and marked.

5 To cut the middle triangles of the star point units, use Template B. Align the template with the edges of the strip of fabric and cut out (1) template shape.

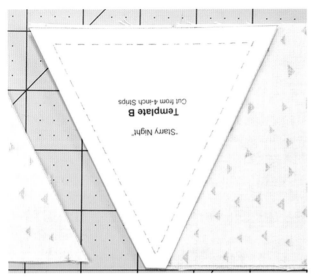

6 Rotate the template on the strip and align one edge with the previous cut. Continue rotating and cutting the template to make additional shapes.

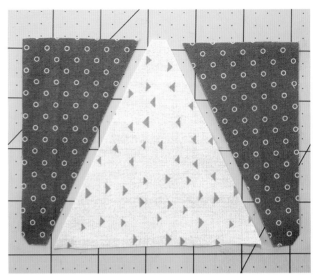

7 To assemble the star points, place a star point and a reverse star point on either side of a background star triangle so that they form a square.

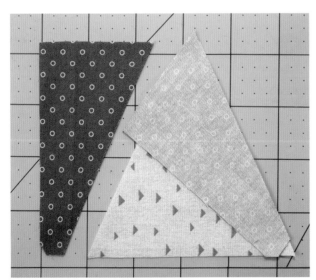

8 Lay one of the star points on top of background triangle and use the trimmed corner to align the (2) pieces. Sew with a ¼" (0.64cm) seam. Press the seams open or to the dark side of the fabric. NOTE: To reduce bulk, press the seams open.

9 Sew a star point to the opposite side in the same manner. Press the seams open or to the dark side of the fabric.

Trimming the Salute to Service Blocks

This example shows you how to make sure your blocks are trimmed to the recommended measurement.

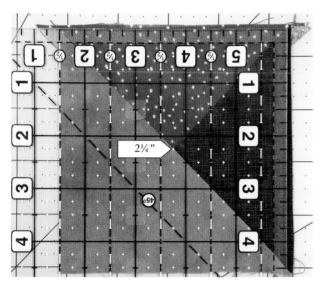

1 To square up these pieces, place a square ruler so that the top and right edges of the ruler are 2¼" (5.72cm) from where the (3) fabrics meet.

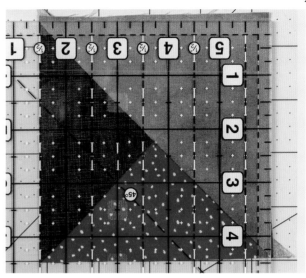

2 Trim the fabric from the right and top edges.

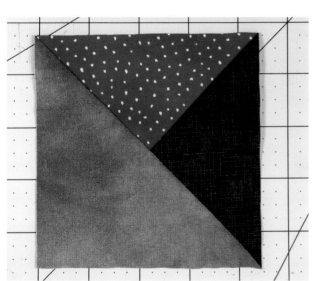

3 Turn the block so that the newly trimmed edges hit the 4½" (11.43cm) lines on the ruler. Again, trim the remaining fabric from the right and top edges for a perfect 4½" (11.43cm) block.

Inspired Star Block Quilts 11

Layering and Basting the Quilt

The process of finishing your quilt involves layering the quilt top with the batting and backing in preparation for quilting.

In order to do this, you must decide on your method of quilting, hand or machine quilt, and the quilting design you wish to use. Once you have determined how you will quilt the piece, you can choose the type of batting that will work best for your quilt. (See page 6, Batting.)

Depending on your chosen quilting method and your quilting design, you may need to mark the design on the quilt top. If you have chosen to quilt in the ditch (stitching close to the seams), or will be doing an all-over quilting pattern with a free-motion technique, marking may not be necessary.

If you do need to mark the design, using a removable marking tool is a good idea. Be sure to test the marker you have chosen on a small scrap of your fabrics to be sure that you can see it well and remove the marking lines when you are finished. (See page 7, Marking Tools, Rulers, and Templates.)

If you will be quilting the quilt yourself, lay the backing wrong side up on a flat surface, smoothing it out as much as possible. Start with a piece of tape in the middle of one edge of the quilt backing, taping it to the surface. Move to the opposite side, smoothing the fabric as you go. Be careful not to stretch the fabric, just make it smooth and flat. Put another piece of tape in the middle of the opposite edge. Repeat this process with the other two sides. Continue working in this fashion from the center of the backing, moving out to the sides and corners until your backing is flat and snug, but not stretched. (If you are working on a carpeted floor, anchor the backing by sticking pins through the edge of the backing right into the carpeting, and anchoring in the same manner as if you were working on a hard surface.)

Before layering the batting, allow it to relax for a day by laying it out flat, or put it in the dryer for few minutes to help smooth out any wrinkles and folds. Center the batting on top of the anchored batting and flatten it out as much as possible. Now you can layer the quilt top onto the backing and batting.

Center the quilt top on the batting. If you plan to hand-quilt the project, baste the project with long lengths of thread every 4"–6" (10.16–15.24cm). Stitch in both directions, forming a grid. I suggest that you use thread that will contrast with the quilt top to make it easy to see. Work from the center of the quilt toward the outside edges, stitching in all directions.

If you plan to quilt your project on your home sewing machine, you will need to pin baste the layers together. Place #2, rust-proof safety pins about every 3"–4" (7.62–10.16cm) across the entire quilt. You will need to pull pins out as you go if they are too close to the presser foot.

Quilt the layers by hand or machine using thread that is appropriate to your quilting design and method. Again, read the label on your thread to be sure you are using a thread that is compatible with your quilting method and sewing machine. (Quilting thread is heavier than machine thread and should not be used in your machine.)

Tips

- Cut the backing fabric and the batting about 4" (10.16cm) larger than the quilt top on all sides. For smaller wall hangings, 2" (5.08cm) may be sufficient.

- Press the backing fabric first to remove any wrinkles and get it as smooth as possible.

- If your backing has been pieced, press your seams to one side to make a stronger seam.

- Remove any threads or other debris (pet hair can be a big issue) from your quilt top and backing. These threads can shadow through lighter fabrics and spoil the look of your beautiful quilt.

- Press your quilt top and make sure that all seams are as flat as possible.

Backing   *Batting*   *Quilt Top*   *Basting Stitches*

Binding the Quilt

A double-fold binding is one of the most common ways to finish a quilt. This method covers the edges of your quilt with two layers of fabric, giving the edge a nice, durable finish.

Measure all four sides of the quilt top to determine the amount of binding needed. Cut enough strips of fabric to completely go around this measurement with at least 12–15" (30.48– 38.10cm) (or more) in excess. Whenever possible, cut the strips across the width of the fabric from the fold to the selvages, to make the binding a little easier to handle. I cut my binding strips to 2¼" (5.72cm) for the binding but 2½" (6.35cm) strips are a common size used by many quilters.

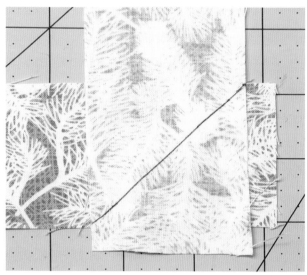

1 Sew the strips together to create one continuous binding strip. Join the strips using diagonal seams. With right sides together, lay the strips out at a right angle and mark a line from one intersection to the other, as shown.

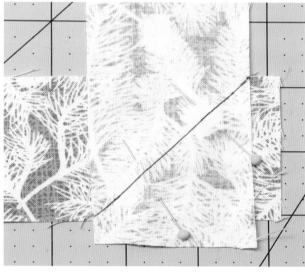

2 Place a couple of pins on either side of the line to keep the pieces in place. Sew on the marked line.

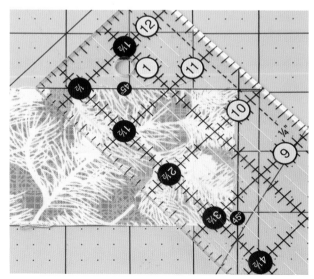

3 Continue adding strips in this manner. Trim one end of the long strip, using the 45° line on a ruler.

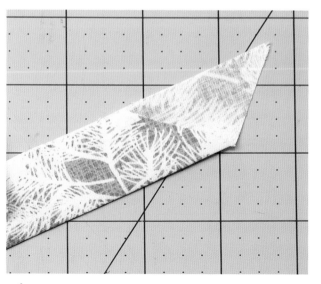

4 Fold the long strip of binding in half, lengthwise, with wrong sides together, (WST), and press.

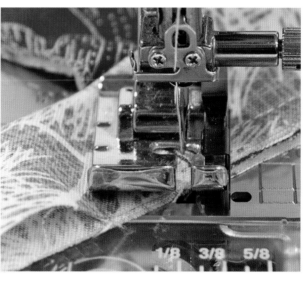

5   Align the raw edges of the binding with the edge of the quilt top. Begin attaching the binding to the quilt, with the angled cut end at least 10"–12" (25.40–30.48cm) from a corner. Take a couple backstitches to secure the thread.

6   As you approach a corner, stop ¼" (0.64cm) away with the needle in the down position. Lift the presser foot and pivot the quilt 45°. The presser foot should be facing away from the corner. Sew to the corner, cut the threads, and remove the quilt from the machine.

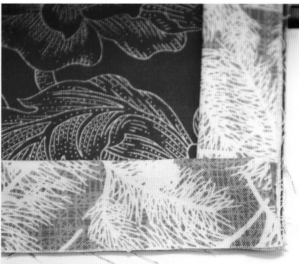

7   Fold the binding back, aligning the binding along the straight line of the quilt and using the 45° sewn line as a guide.

8   Fold the binding back down on itself, aligning the raw edge of the binding with the edge of the quilt top on the next side.

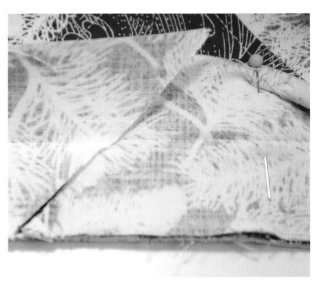

9 Place the quilt top back under the presser foot and sew to the next corner. Repeat step 6–8 at each corner. Stop within 10"–15" (25.40–38.10cm) of the beginning of the sewn binding.

10 To join the ends of the binding, lay the quilt on a flat surface. Open up the end of binding and smooth it so it lays flat on the quilt top. Open the beginning end, the end with the angled cut, and smooth it out on top of the ending. This helps determine where to place the joining seam. Secure with a pin or two to keep it in place.

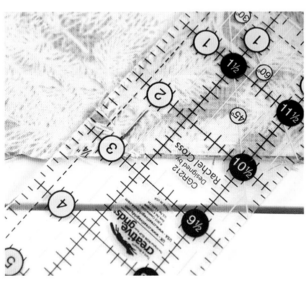

11 Making sure that the quilt and binding pieces are completely flat, make a mark on the ending binding piece, along the angled cut, as shown. Remove the pins, pull aside the angled end of the binding. and align the 45° line of a ruler along the edge of the strip.

12 Move the edge of the ruler ½" (1.27cm) from the first mark. Make sure that the new line is marked in the same direction as the cut on the starting end. Cut the strip at the new marked diagonal line.

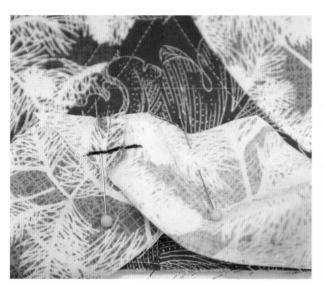

13 Match the 45° cuts from each end, placing right sides together. Pin the pieces together.

14 Sew the ends together using a ¼" (0.64cm) seam. Press the seam open. Refold the binding in half and realign along the edge of the quilt. Sew the binding in place to finish attaching it to the quilt.

Labeling the Quilt

Your quilt is not complete until you add a label.

Identify the name of the quilt, who the quilt is for, if it is to be a gift, start and/or finish dates, your name, the recipient's name, the occasion (such as a birthday or anniversary), and any information that might be important to remember about the quilt.

"Crossing Boundaries"

An original quilt designed, pieced and machine quilted by Sandy Berg for Raspberry Bramble Designs

Pattern # RBD105

Started November 2018
Completed December 2018

Projects

Oh My Stars! 20

Providence 28

Point the Way 56

Starburst 64

Salute to Service 82

Fandango Dance 88

Star Chain 36

Star Crossing 42

Starry Night 70

Window on the Stars 76

In Honor 96

Stars of the Show 102

Materials

- 2¾ yards (251.46cm) background fabric
- ½ yard (45.72cm) red-orange fabric
- ⅜ yard (34.29cm) light turquoise fabric
- 1⅝ yards (148.59cm) charcoal fabric
- ⅜ yard (34.29cm) dark turquoise fabric
- ¼ yard (22.86cm) gold fabric
- 4½ yards (411.48cm) batting and backing fabric
- ⅝ yard (57.15cm) binding fabric

Oh My Stars!

Stars, within stars, within stars. This quilt says "patriotic" all the way. Could there be a better way to say "I love America" than this?

Cutting Instructions

NOTE: Keep the pieces organized by size to make construction easier.

From the background fabric, cut:
(2) 9" (22.86cm) x WOF strips, from the strips, cut:
    (6) 9" (22.86cm) squares
(1) 8½" (21.59cm) x WOF strip, from the strip, cut:
    (4) 8½" (21.59cm) squares
(1) 5¼" (13.34cm) x WOF strip, from the strip, cut:
    (6) 5¼" (13.34cm) squares
(2) 4½" (11.43cm) x WOF strips, from the strips, cut:
    (4) 4½" x 6½" (11.43 x 16.51cm) rectangles
    (4) 4½" (11.43cm) squares
(2) 3" (7.62cm) x WOF strips, from the strips, cut:
    (16) 3" (7.62cm) squares
(12) 2½" (6.35cm) x WOF strips, from (9) strips, cut:
    (4) 2½" x 32½" (6.35 x 82.55cm) strips
    (8) 2½" x 8½" (6.35 x 21.59cm) rectangles
    (28) 2½" (6.35cm) squares
    (1) 2½" x 11" (6.35 x 27.94cm) strip, reserve the remaining (3) strips
(6) 2" (5.08cm) x WOF strip
(3) 1½" (3.81cm) x WOF strips

From the red-orange fabric, cut:
(1) 9" (22.86cm) x WOF strip, from the strip, cut:
    (2) 9" (22.86cm) squares
(1) 3" (7.62cm) x WOF strip, from the strip, cut:
    (4) 3" (7.62cm) squares
(1) 2⅞" (7.30cm) x WOF strip, from the strip, cut:
    (8) 2⅞" (7.30cm) squares

From the charcoal fabric, cut:
(7) 5½" (13.97cm) x WOF strips.
(1) 5" (12.7cm) x WOF strip, from the strip, cut:
    (4) 5" (12.7cm) squares
(1) 3" (7.62cm) x WOF strip, from the strip, cut:
    (12) 3" (7.62cm) squares
(1) 2⅞" (7.30cm) x WOF strip, from the strip, cut:
    (16) 2⅞" (7.30cm) squares
(3) 1½" (3.81cm) x WOF strips

From the dark turquoise fabric, cut:
(1) 9" (22.86cm) x WOF strip, from the strip, cut:
    (4) 9" (22.86cm) squares
(1) 2½" (6.35cm) x WOF strip, from the strip, cut:
    (1) 2½" x 22" (6.35 x 55.88cm) strip

From the gold fabric, cut:
(1) 4½" (11.43cm) x WOF strip, from the strip, cut:
    (1) 4½" (11.43cm) square
    (1) 2½" x 22" (6.35 x 55.88cm) strip

From the light turquoise fabric, cut:
(1) 5" (12.7cm) x WOF strip, from the strip, cut:
    (4) 5" (12.7cm) squares
(1) 4½" (11.43cm) x WOF strip, from the strip, cut:
    (4) 4½" (11.43cm) squares
(1) 2½" x 11" (6.35 x 27.94cm) strip

From the binding fabric, cut:
(7) strips 2¼" (5.72cm) x WOF strips

Pieced by Shelley Nagle, Lewiston, Idaho
Quilted by Sandy Berg
Finished Quilt: 61" x 71" (154.94 x 180.34cm)

Making the Blocks

Draw a diagonal line on the wrong side of:
- (16) 3" (7.62cm) background fabric squares
- (4) 5" (12.7cm) light turquoise squares
- (6) 9" (22.86cm) background squares
- (8) 2⅞" (7.30cm) red-orange squares

Central Stars – Small, Medium, and Large

For the blocks in the center of the quilt, press the seams open. Since there will be many seams that meet and lay on one another, reducing bulk will make the quilt center lay flatter.

1. Place a marked 3" (7.62cm) background square on top of a 3" (7.62cm) red-orange square, RST. Sew ¼" (0.64cm) away from both sides of the diagonal line. Cut in half on the diagonal line and press the seams open. Trim to 2½" (6.35cm) square. Make (8) HSTs.

Make 8

2. Sew the HSTs together in sets of (2), as shown, to make (4) paired HST units. Press the seams open.

Make 4

3. Sew a 2½" (6.35cm) background square to each end of (2) red-orange paired HSTs, as shown, to make (2) star point rows. Press the seams open.

Make 2

4. Using a 4½" (11.43cm) gold square for the center, sew a unit from step 2 to two sides of the square, as shown. Press the seams open.

5. Sew a star point row to the top and bottom of the unit made in step 4 to complete a small center star. Press the seams open. The unit should measure 8½" (21.59cm) square.

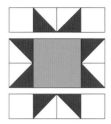 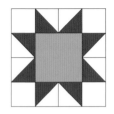

6. Place a marked 5" (12.7cm) light turquoise square on top of a 5" (12.7cm) charcoal square, RST. Sew ¼" (0.64cm) away from both sides of the diagonal line. Cut in half on the diagonal line and press the seams open. Trim to 4½" (11.43cm) square. Make (8) HSTs.

Make 8

7. Sew the HSTs together in sets of (2), as shown, to make (4) paired HST units. Press the seams open.

Make 4

8. Sew a 4½" (11.43cm) light turquoise square to the end of (2) of the paired HSTs, as shown, to make (2) star point rows. Press the seams open.

Make 2

9. Sew a paired, light turquoise/charcoal HST to opposite sides of the small center star from step 5. Press the seams open.

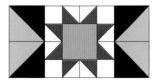

10. Sew a star point row to the top and bottom of the step 9 unit to make a medium center star. Press the seams open. The square should measure 16½" (41.91cm).

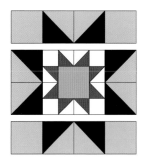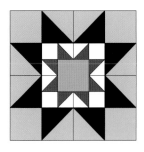

11. Place a marked 9" (22.86cm) background square on top of a 9" (22.86cm) dark turquoise square, RST. Sew ¼" (0.64cm) away from both sides of the diagonal line. Cut in half on the diagonal line and press the seams open. Make (8) HSTs. The squares should measure 8½" (21.59cm).

Make 8

12. Sew the HSTs together in sets of (2), as shown, to make (4) paired HST units. Press the seams open.

Make 4

13. Sew an 8½" (21.59cm) background square to each end of (2) of the paired HSTs, as shown, to make (2) star point rows. Press the seams open.

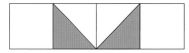

Make 2

14. Sew a paired, dark turquoise/background HST to opposite sides of the center star from step 10. Press the seams open.

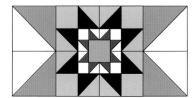

15. Sew a star point row to the top and bottom of the step 14 unit to make a large center star. Press the seams open. The square should measure 32½" (82.55cm).

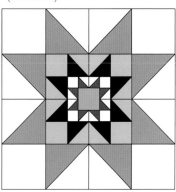

Pinwheel Side Sections

1. Place a marked 3" (7.62cm) background square on top of a 3" (7.62cm) charcoal square, RST. Sew ¼" (0.64cm) away from both sides of the diagonal line. Cut in half on the diagonal line and press the seams open. Trim to 2½" (6.35cm) square. Make (24) HSTs.

Make 24

2. Lay out (2) HSTs from step 1, as shown. Sew together, using a ¼" (0.64cm) seam. Press the seams open. Make (12) 2½" x 4½" (6.35 x 11.43cm) units.

Make 12

3. Sew together (2) units from step 2 to make a pinwheel. Press the seams open. Make (6) 4½" (11.43cm) pinwheel blocks.

Make 6

4. Sew a 4½" (11.43cm) background square to (4) pinwheels. Press the seams open. Make (4) end pinwheels.

Make 4

5. On the (2) remaining pinwheels, sew a 4½" x 6½" (11.43 x 16.51cm) background rectangle to opposite sides of the pinwheels and press the seams open. Make (2) middle pinwheels.

Make 2

6. Sew an end pinwheel on both ends of a middle pinwheel, as shown. Make sure the seam aligns along the edge of the pinwheel. Press the seams open. Make (2) pinwheel strips.

Make 2

Making the Top and Bottom Rows

NOTE: Seams should now be pressed as instructed.

1. Place a marked 9" (22.86cm) background square on top of a 9" (22.86cm) red-orange square. Sew ¼" (0.64cm) away from both sides of the diagonal line. Cut in half on the line to make (2) 8½" (21.59cm) HSTs. Press the seams toward the red-orange. Trim to 8½" (21.59cm) square. Repeat to make a total of (4) corner HSTs.

Make 4

2. Sew the (3) 1½" (3.81cm) x WOF background strips using diagonal seams. Repeat with the (3) 1½" (3.81cm) x WOF of charcoal strips. Sew the strips together to make (1) background/charcoal strip set.

Make 1

3. Sew a 2½" x 11" (6.35 x 27.94cm) light turquoise strip to a 2½" x 11" (6.35 x 27.94cm) background strip. Press the seam toward the light turquoise. Cut the strip set into (4) 2½" x 4½" (6.35 x 11.43cm) segments.

Cut 4 segments

4. Sew together (2) segments from step 3 to make a four-patch. Press the seam in either direction. Make (2) 4½" (11.43cm) four-patch units.

Make 2

5. Sew a 2½" x 22" (6.35 x 55.88cm) dark turquoise strip to a 2½" x 22" (6.35 x 55.88cm) gold strip. Press the seam toward the dark turquoise. Cut the strip set into (8) 2½" x 4½" (6.35 x 11.43cm) segments.

Cut 8 segments

6. Sew together (2) segments from step 5 to make a four-patch. Press the seam in either direction. Make (4) 4½" (11.43cm) four-patch units.

Make 4

7. To make Four-at-a-time Flying Geese units, place (2) 2⅞" (7.30cm) marked red-orange squares on opposite corners of a 5¼" (13.34cm) background square, RST. (The smaller squares will overlap slightly in the center.) Sew ¼" (0.64cm) seam on each side of the marked line.

8. Fold the smaller triangles away from the background triangle. Press the seams toward the smaller triangles.

9. With RST, place a marked, 2⅞" (7.30cm) red-orange square on the background triangle corner of one unit from step 8. Sew ¼" (0.64cm) seam on each side of the marked line. Cut in half on the line, and press the seam toward the small triangle. Repeat with the other triangle unit to make (4) Flying Geese units. Trim to 2½" x 4½" (6.35 x 11.43cm) to make (8), Flying Geese units.

Make 8

10. Repeat steps 7–9 to make a total of (16) Flying Geese units from the background/charcoal fabric.

Make 16

11. Lay out (4) 2½" (6.35cm) background fabric squares, (4) charcoal Flying Geese, and (1) #2, four-patch, as shown. Sew the units into (3) rows. In the top and bottom rows, press the seams toward the outside, and in the middle row, press to the four-patch. Sew the rows together and press the seams to the outside. Repeat to make (4) #1 star blocks. Trim to 8½" (21.59cm).

12. Lay out (4) 2½" (6.35cm) background fabric squares, (4) red-orange Flying Geese, and (1) #1, four-patch, as shown. Sew the units into (3) rows. In the top and bottom rows, press the seams toward the outside, and in the middle row, press to the four-patch. Sew the rows together and press the seams to the outside. Repeat to make (2) #2 star blocks. Trim to 8½" (21.59cm).

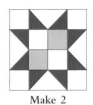

Make 2

Make 4

13. Lay out (2) red-orange corner HSTs, (2) star #1 blocks, and (1) #2 star block, with (4) 2½" x 8½" (6.35 x 21.59cm) background fabric rectangles. Place (1) sashing strip between each of the blocks. Sew together and press the seams toward the sashing strips. Repeat to make (2) rows.

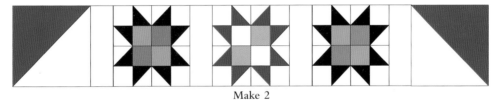

Make 2

14. Measure the row from step 13 through the center width. Cut (2) segments from the charcoal/background strip set from step 2, equal to this measurement. Sew a segment to each of the rows, as shown below. Press the seams toward the background fabric.

15. Sew the (3) remaining 2½" (6.35cm) x WOF background fabric strips into a long strip using diagonal seams. Cut (2) strips equal to the same measurement from step 14, and sew a segment to each of the rows, as shown. Press the seams toward the background fabric. Make (2) rows.

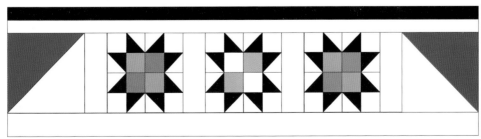

Make 2

Assembling the Quilt Center

1. Sew a 2½" x 32½" (6.35 x 82.55cm) background strip to the top and bottom of a pinwheel section. Press the seams open. Repeat to make (2) pinwheel units.

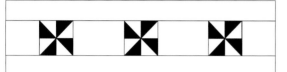

Make 2

2. Sew a pinwheel strip to opposite sides of the large central star to complete the middle star section of the quilt. Press the seams open.

3. Sew the top and bottom rows to the middle star section of the quilt and press the seams toward the outer background strips, away from the middle star section.

Adding the Borders

1. Sew together (6) 2" (5.08cm) x WOF background strips with diagonal seams. Measure the quilt length through the center of the quilt. Cut (2) side border sections from the long strip, equal to the length measurement. Sew the border sections to each side of the quilt center, pressing seams to the outside.

2. Measure the quilt width through the center of the quilt, including the side borders. Cut (2) border strips equal to the width measurement. Sew to the top and bottom of the quilt, pressing seams to the outside.

3. Sew the (7) 5½" (13.97cm) x WOF charcoal strips together, joining them on the diagonal. Repeat steps 1 and 2 to add outer borders to the quilt center. Press the seams to the outside.

Finishing the Quilt

1. Layer the backing, batting, and quilt top. Baste and quilt as desired.

2. Sew (7) 2¼" (5.72cm) x WOF binding fabric strips together, joining them with diagonal seams. Refer to Binding the Quilt, pages 14–17, for binding instructions

Providence

These stars appear to be hanging on a trellis, and they are contained in the garden by a lovely fence. What a garden this would make! Jason Yenter's "Unusual Garden" line is a perfect setting for this beautiful quilt.

Materials

- 2½ yards (228.60cm) white background fabric
- 1¾ yards (160.02cm) black floral fabric for blocks
- ½ yard (45.72cm) fuchsia fabric for star centers and border
- ⅛ yard (11.43cm) yellow fabric for star centers
- ½ yard (45.72cm) dark turquoise fabric for star points
- ⅝ yard (57.15cm) light turquoise fabric for stars
- ⅛ yard (11.43cm) dark gray for fabric sashing cornerstones
- ¾ yard (68.58cm) light gray fabric for sashing
- ⅞ yard (80.01cm) green fabric for block sashing
- 1¼ yards (114.3cm) black fabric for border
- 5¾ yards (525.78cm) batting and backing fabric
- ¾ yard (68.58cm) for binding

Cutting Instructions

From the white background fabric, cut:
(3) 8" (20.32cm) x WOF strips,
from the strips, cut:
(8) 8" (20.32cm) squares
(2) 5½" (13.97cm) squares
(2) 5½" (13.97cm) x WOF strips
(4) 3½" (8.89cm) x WOF strips,
from the strips, cut:
(36) 3½" (8.89cm) squares
(12) 3" (7.62cm) x WOF strips,
from the strips, cut:
(60) 3" (7.62cm) squares
(8) 3" x 10½" (7.62 x 26.67cm) strips
(10) 3" x 13" (7.62 x 33.02cm) strips

From the black floral fabric, cut:
(4) 13" (33.02cm) x WOF strips,
from the strips, cut:
(12) 13" (33.02cm) squares
(1) 8" (20.32cm) x WOF strip,
from the strip, cut:
(2) 8" x 13" (20.32 x 33.02cm) strips

From the green fabric, cut:
(2) 5½" (13.97cm) x WOF strips,
from the strips, cut:
(8) 5½" (13.97cm) squares
(5) 3" (7.62cm) x WOF strips,
from the strips, cut:
(8) 3" x 8" (7.62 x 20.32cm) strips
(8) 3" x 10½" (7.62 x 26.67cm) strips
(2) 3" x 13" (7.62 x 33.02cm) strips

From the dark gray fabric, cut:
(1) 3" (7.62cm) x WOF strip,
from the strip, cut:
(1) 3" x 20" (7.62 x 50.8cm) strip

From the light gray fabric, cut:
(1) 5½" (13.97cm) x WOF strip,
from the strip, cut:
(2) 5½" x 20" (13.97cm x 50.8cm) strips
(1) 4" (11.43cm) x WOF strip,
from the strip, cut:
(9) 4" (10.16cm) squares
(5) 3" (7.62cm) x WOF strips,
from (4) strips, cut:
(36) 3" (7.62cm) squares
(1) 3" x 5½" (7.62 x 13.97cm) strip,
reserve remaining strip

From the dark turquoise fabric, cut:
(4) 3½" (8.89cm) x WOF strips,
from the strips, cut:
(36) 3½" (8.89cm) squares

From light turquoise fabric, cut:
(2) 4" (10.16cm) x WOF strips,
from the strips, cut:
(18) 4" (10.16cm) squares
(3) 3" (7.62cm) x WOF strips, from the strips, cut:
(36) 3" (7.62cm) squares

From the yellow fabric, cut:
(1) 3" (7.62cm) x WOF strip,
from the strip, cut:
(9) 3" (7.62cm) squares

From the fuchsia fabric, cut:
(8) 1¼" (3.18cm) x WOF strips
(1) 4" (10.16cm) x WOF strip,
from the strip, cut:
(9) 4" (11.43cm) squares

From the black fabric, cut:
(9) 4½" (12.7cm) x WOF strips

From the binding fabric, cut:
(9) 2¼" (5.72cm) x WOF strips

Pieced by Sharon Ledbetter, Clarkston, WA
Quilted by Sandy Berg
Finished Quilt: 70"x 95" (177.8 x 241.3cm)

Making the Blocks

1. Draw a diagonal line on the back of the following squares:
   - (36) 3½" (8.89cm) white background squares
   - (24) 3" (7.62cm) white background squares
   - (8) 5½" (13.97cm) green squares
   - (18) 4" (10.16cm) light turquoise squares

2. Layer a marked 3½" (8.89cm) background square on top of a 3½" (8.89cm) dark turquoise square. Sew ¼" (0.64cm) on both sides of the drawn line. Cut on the drawn line. Press the seam toward the dark fabric. Trim to 3" (7.62cm) to make (72) half-square triangles.

Make 72

3. Sew a HST from step 2, to the right side of a 3" (7.62cm) background square. Pay attention to the orientation of the HST. Sew and press seam to the HST. Make (36) HST/square units.

Make 36

4. Repeat step 3, sewing a light turquoise 3" (7.62cm) square to the right side of a HST from step 2, paying attention to orientation Press the seam to the HST. Make (36) HST/square units.

Make 36

5. Sew the units from steps 3 and 4 together, as shown, to make (36) star points. Press the seams toward the light turquoise.

Make 36

6. Layer (9) marked 4" (10.16cm) light turquoise squares on top of (9) 4" (10.16cm) fuchsia squares. Sew ¼" (0.64cm) on either side of the drawn line. Cut on the drawn line and press seams towards the dark fabric. Make (18) light turquoise/fuchsia triangles. Cut these triangles in half across the seam line to make (36) smaller triangle units.

Make 18   **Make 36**

7. Repeat step 6, sewing (9) marked 4" (10.16cm) light turquoise squares on top of (9) 4" (10.16cm) light gray squares. Sew ¼" (0.64cm) on either side of the drawn line. Cut on the drawn line and press seams to one side. Make (18) light turquoise/light gray triangles. Cut the triangles in half across the seam line to make (36) smaller triangle units.

Make 18   **Make 36**

8. Sew together one of each of the triangle units from steps 6–7 on the long side. Press the seam toward the light turquoise/fuchsia side. Make (36). Hourglass blocks. Trim the units to 3" (7.62cm). Add a 3" (7.62cm) square of light gray to the Hourglass block, matching the light gray triangle, as shown. Press the seam toward the square. Make (36) units.

Make 36

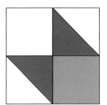

9. Sew a star point to each side of (18) Hourglass blocks from step 8. Press the seams toward the star points to make (18) half star units.

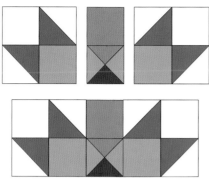

Make 18

10. Add an Hourglass block to each side of a 3" (7.62cm) yellow square. Press the seams toward the yellow square. Make (9) joining units.

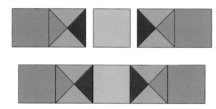

Make 9

11. Sew a half star unit to the top and bottom of a joining unit from step 10. Press seam toward the outside to complete the Providence block. The blocks should measure 13" (33.02cm). Make (9) blocks.

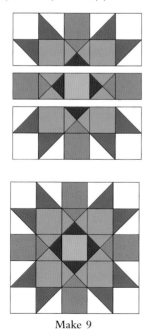

Make 9

Making the Alternate Blocks

1. Make a strip set by sewing a 5½" x 20" (13.97 x 50.8cm) strip of light gray to each ide of a 3" x 20" (7.62 x 50.8cm) dark gray trip. Press the seams toward light gray. From the strip set, cut (4) segments measuring 3" (7.62cm) wide.

Cut 4 segments

2. Make a second strip set by sewing a 5½" (13.97cm) x WOF strip of background fabric to each side of a 3" (7.62cm) x WOF strip of light gray. Press the seams toward the light gray. From the strip set, cut (7) segments measuring 5½" (13.97cm) wide.

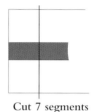

Cut 7 segments

3. Sew a 5½" (13.97cm) square of background fabric to each side of a 3" x 5½" (7.62 x 13.97cm) strip of light gray to make an additional segment from step 2. Press the seams toward the light gray.

4. Sew a segment from step 2 to both sides of a segment from step 1, as shown. Press the seams toward the middle of the block to make (4) alternate blocks. Trim to 13" (33.02cm) square.

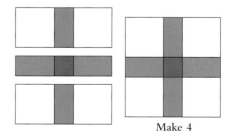

Make 4

Making Edging Blocks

1. On the top of (8) 3" x 8" (7.62 x 20.32cm) green strips, place a marked 3" (7.62cm) background square so that the diagonal line goes from bottom left to top right. Sew on the marked line. Trim the corner, leaving a ¼" (0.64cm) seam allowance. Press the seam allowance toward the green strip. Make (8) units.

Make 8

2. On the top of (8) 3" x 10½" (7.62 x 26.67cm) green strips, place a marked 3" (7.62cm) background square so that the diagonal line goes from the upper left corner to the lower right corner. Sew on the marked line. Trim the corner, leaving a ¼" (0.64cm) seam allowance. Press the seam allowance toward the green strip. Make (8) units.

Make 8

3. Sew an 8" (20.32cm) strip from step 1 to the right side of an 8" (20.32cm) background square, right sides together. Press the seam toward the 8" (20.32cm) square.

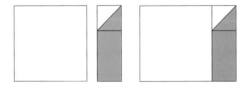

4. Sew a unit from step 2 to the bottom of the square from step 3, as shown. Press the seam to the outside.

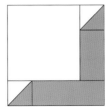

5. To complete the edging blocks, sew a 3" x 10½" (7.62 x 26.67cm) background strip to the top, pressing seams to the outside. Sew a 3" x 13" (7.62 x 33.02cm) background strip to the left side of the block, pressing seams to the outside. Make (8) blocks. Square the blocks to 13" (33.02cm).

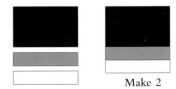

Make 8

6. Place a marked 5½" (13.97cm) green square on one corner of a 13" (33.02cm) square of floral fabric. Sew on the marked line, and trim the corner, leaving a ¼" (0.64cm) seam allowance. Press the seam toward the green fabric.

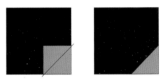

7. Sew a marked 3" (7.62cm) background square to the green corner, as shown. Press the seam toward the green fabric. Make (8) edging corner blocks. Square to 13" (33.02cm).

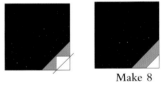

Make 8

8. Sew a 3" x 13" (7.62 x 33.02cm) green strip to the bottom of an 8" x 13" (20.32 x 33.02cm) floral rectangle, pressing seams toward the green strip. Sew a 3" x 13" (7.62 x 33.02cm) background strip to the bottom of the green strip, pressing seams toward the background fabric. Repeat to make a second block. Square to 13" (33.02cm).

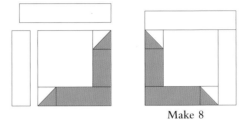

Make 2

Making the Quilt Center

1. Using the Quilt Assembly Diagram, lay out the blocks as shown and sew together to make rows.

2. Press the seams in odd numbered rows in one direction, and even number rows in the opposite direction.

3. Sew the rows together. The seams will nest as the rows are sewn.

Quilt Assembly Diagram

Adding the Borders

1. Sew the 1¼" (3.18cm) x WOF fuchsia border strips together, joining them with diagonal seams. Measure the quilt length through the center of the quilt. Cut two side border sections from the long strip, equal to the length measurement. Sew the border sections to each side of the quilt center, pressing seams to the outside.

2. Measure the quilt width through the center of the quilt including the side borders. Cut 2 border strips equal to the width measurement. Sew to the top and bottom of the quilt pressing seams to the outside.

3. Sew the 4½" (12.7cm) x WOF black strips together, joining them on the diagonal. Repeat steps 1 and 2 to add outer borders to the quilt center.

Finishing the Quilt

1. Layer, baste, and quilt as desired.

2. Sew (9) 2¼" (5.72cm) x WOF binding strips together, joining them with diagonal seams. Refer to Binding the Quilt, pages 14–17, for binding instructions.

Star Chain

A beautiful Star block is the focus of this quilt! The alternate block provides a link that connects the stars as they march across the quilt diagonally. The use of two medium blues helps make them sparkle.

Materials

- 2⅜ yards (217.17cm) for white fabric for background
- ¼ yard (22.86cm) pale yellow fabric for four-patch blocks
- 1⅞ yards (171.45cm) light blue fabric for four-patch blocks and borders
- ¾ yard (68.58cm) #1 medium blue fabric for star blocks
- ⅝ yard (57.15cm) #2 medium blue fabric for star blocks
- ½ yard (45.72cm) dark blue fabric for four-patch blocks and star blocks
- 5 yards (457.20cm) batting and backing fabric
- ¾ yard (68.58cm) binding fabric

- Optional Tool: Tri-Recs Tool™ by Darlene Zimmerman and Joy Hoffman

- Star Point Templates (page 108)

Cutting Instructions

From the white background fabric, cut:
(15) 5½" (13.97cm) x WOF strips, from (12) strips, cut:
   (12) 5½" x 15½" (13.97 x 39.37cm) rectangles
   (20) 5½" x 10½" (13.97 x 26.67cm) rectangles
   (20) 5½" (13.97cm) squares,
   reserve the (3) additional strips for later use

From the dark blue fabric, cut:
(5) 3" (7.62cm) x WOF trips

From #1 medium blue fabric, cut:
(2) 5½" (13.97cm) x WOF strips
(8) 1½" (3.81cm) x WOF inner border strips

From #2 medium blue fabric, cut:
(2) 5½" (13.97cm) x WOF strips
(2) 3" (7.62cm) x WOF strips

From the light blue fabric, cut:
(8) 3" (7.62cm) x WOF strips, from 3 strips, cut:
   (20) 3" x 5½" (7.62 x 13.97cm) rectangles,
   reserve (5) strips to make strip sets
(9) 4½" (11.43cm) x WOF strips for outer border

From the yellow fabric, cut:
(2) 3" (7.62cm) x WOF

From the binding fabric, cut:
(9) 2¼" (5.72cm) x WOF strips

Pieced and Quilted by Kelly McKeehan, Lewiston, Idaho
Finished Quilt: 70" x 85" (177.8 x 215.9cm)

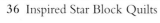

Making the Strip Sets

1. For strip set #1 (SS1), sew a 3" (7.62cm) strip of light blue to a 3" (7.62cm) strip of dark blue, RST. Press the seam to the dark blue. The strip should measure 5½" (13.97cm) x WOF. Make (3) strip sets and subcut them into (40) 3" (7.62cm) segments. If you need one more segment, use leftover fabric to cut a 3" (7.62cm) square of light blue and dark blue. Sew the squares together to make an additional segment.

Make 3 SS1; cut 40 segments

2. For strip set #2 (SS2), sew a 3" (7.62cm) strip of medium blue to a 3" (7.62cm) strip of dark blue, RST. Press the seam to the dark blue. The strip should measure 5½" (13.97cm) x WOF. Make two strip sets and subcut them into (20) 3" (7.62cm) segments.

Make 2 SS2; cut 20 segments

3. For strip set #3 (SS3), sew a 3" (7.62cm) strip of yellow to a 3" (7.62cm) strip of light blue, RST. Press the seam open. The strip should measure 5½" (13.97cm) x WOF. Make (2) strip sets and subcut them into (20) 3" (7.62cm) segments.

Make 3 SS3; cut 20 segments

Making the Star Points

NOTE: This pattern includes templates (page 108) to make the star points for the stars in the center of the quilt. Refer to pages 8–10, Making Elongated Star Points, for instructions.

1. Place (2) #1 medium blue, 5½" (13.97cm) x WOF strips, RST. Using Template A, align the bottom of the template with the bottom of the strips. Cut out (1) template shape.

2. Rotate Template A, placing the template bottom on the top edge of the strip, and cut another shape. Continue rotating the template and cutting out the shapes. You will end up with one shape that is the reverse of the other for each shape you cut. Keep the (2) shapes separated and marked. Cut (20) of each shape.

Cut 20 of each shape

3. Repeat steps 1 and 2, using (2) strips of #2 medium blue to make (20) of each shape.

Cut 20 of each shape

4. From each of (3) strips of 5½" (13.97cm) x WOF background fabric, align Template B with the top and bottom of the strip. Cut out (1) template shape by cutting on both sides of the template. Rotate the template on the strip, aligning one edge with the previous cut. Cut the other side to complete another triangle. Continue rotating the template and cut (40) background star triangles.

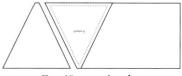

Cut 40 star triangles

5. To make the star points, lay out a #1 medium blue point and a #2 medium blue reverse point on both sides of a background star triangle so that they form a square.

6. Lay (1) of the points on top of the background triangle and sew with a scant ¼" (0.64cm) seam. Press the seam open. Sew the other point to the other side and press the seam open to complete a star point unit. Make (20) star point units with the medium blues in the same order. Trim the units to 5½" (13.97cm) square.

Make 20

7. Repeat step 6 to make (20) star point units, reversing the position of the (2) medium blues, as shown. Trim to 5½" (13.97cm) square.

Make 20

Making the Star Blocks

1. Lay out (2) SS1 segments (page 38), as shown. With RST, sew the segments together. Press the seam open. Make (20) #1, four-patch units. They should measure 5½" (13.97cm) square. Trim to 5½" (13.97cm) square.

Make 20 #1 four-patches

2. Lay out (2) SS2 segments as shown. With RST, sew the segments together. Press seams to one side. Make (10) #2, four-patch units. They should measure 5½" (13.97cm) square. Trim to 5½" (13.97cm) square.

Make 10 #2 four-patches

3. Lay out (2) of each of the star points, (2) #1 four-patch units, (1) #2 four-patch unit, and (2) 5½" (13.97cm) squares of background, as shown.

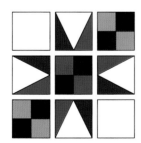

4. Sew the units into (3) rows. Press the seams of the top and bottom row toward the outside, and the middle row to the center. Sew the rows together

and press the seams toward the outside. Make (10) star blocks. The star blocks should measure 15½" (39.37cm) square.

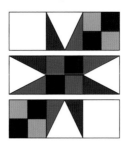
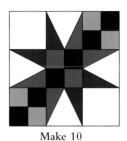

Make 10

Making Alternate Blocks

1. Sew a 3" x 5½" (7.62 x 13.97cm) rectangle of light blue to an SS3 segment, as shown. Press to the light blue. Make (20) units.

Make 20

2. To the bottom of these units, sew a 5½" x 10½" (13.97 x 26.67cm) background rectangle, as shown. Press the seams toward the background rectangle. The rectangles should measure 5½" x 15½" (13.97 x 39.37cm).

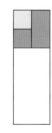

3. Sew (2) of the units from step 2 to both sides of a 5½"x 15½" (13.97 x 39.37cm) background rectangle, as shown. Press the seams toward the background rectangle. Make (10) alternate blocks. The blocks should measure 15½" (39.37cm) square.

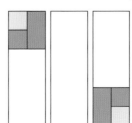
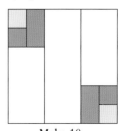

Make 10

Finishing the Quilt Center

1. Following the Quilt Assembly Diagram, lay out the blocks in rows.

2. Sew the blocks into rows. Press the seams toward the alternate blocks. Sew the rows together and press all the seams in the same direction.

Adding the Borders

1. Sew the 1½" (3.81cm) x WOF medium blue #1 strips together, joining them with diagonal seams. Measure the quilt length through the center of the quilt. Cut (2) side border sections from the long strip, equal to the length measurement. Sew the border sections to each side of the quilt center, pressing seams to the outside.

2. Measure the quilt width through the center of the quilt including the side borders. Cut (2) border strips equal to the width measurement. Sew to the top and bottom of the quilt, pressing seams to the outside.

3. Sew the 4¼" (10.79cm) x WOF light blue strips together, joining them on the diagonal. Repeat steps 1 and 2 to add outer borders to the quilt center.

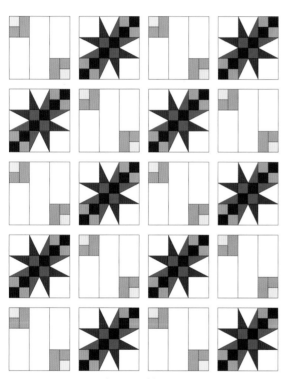

Quilt Assembly Diagram

Finishing the Quilt

1. Layer, baste, and quilt as desired.

2. Sew (9) 2¼" (5.72cm) x WOF binding fabric strips together, joining them with diagonal seams. Refer to Binding the Quilt, pages 14–17, for binding instructions.

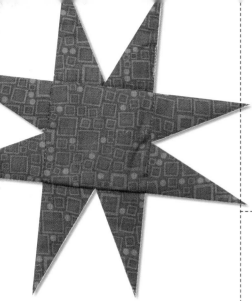

Star Crossing
Lap Size

This quilt is constructed from a block called "Bonnie Scotsman." Four of the units are put together with a "connector" fabric to make up the block for the quilt. Stars in the quilt are formed in the joining sections of the sashing.

Materials

- ⅝ yard (57.15cm) light colors for fabric A
- 1½ yards (137.16cm) light colors for fabric B
- ¾ yard (68.58cm) medium or dark colors for fabric C
- 1⅛ yards (102.87cm) medium or dark colors for fabric D
- ¼ yard (22.86cm) for star fabric
- 1⅛ yards (102.87cm) for outer border
- ½ yard (45.72cm) for block connector fabric
- 5 yards (457.20cm) batting and backing fabric
- ⅝ yard (57.15cm) for binding
- Star Point Templates (page 109)

Cutting Instructions

NOTE: Keep fabric cuts organized by color and size.

From fabric A, cut:
(5) 3½" (8.89cm) x WOF strips

From fabric B, cut:
(6) 2½" (6.35cm) x WOF strips, set aside for strip sets
(9) 2½" (6.35cm) x WOF strips, from the strips, cut:
      (17) 2½" x 15½" (6.35 x 39.37cm) segments,
      from the leftover 2½" (6.35cm) strip, cut:
      (12) 1½" (3.81cm) block joining squares
(7) 2" (5.08cm) x WOF strips for inner borders

From fabric C, cut:
(3) 3½" (8.89cm) x WOF strips
(5) 2½" (6.35cm) x WOF strips

From fabric D, cut:
(3) 5½" (13.97cm) x WOF strips
(8) 2½" (6.35cm) x WOF strips, from the strips, cut:
      (48) 2½" x 5½" (6.35 x 13.97cm) rectangles

From the block connector fabric, cut:
(10) 1½" (3.81cm) x WOF strips, from the strips, cut:
      (48) 1½" x 7½" (3.81 x 19.05cm) rectangles

From the star fabric, cut:
(1) 2½" (6.35cm) x WOF strip, from the strip, cut:
      (6) 2½" (6.35cm) squares
(2) 2⅞" (7.30cm) x WOF strips for star points

From outer border fabric, cut:
(8) 4½" (11.43cm) x WOF strips

From binding fabric, cut:
(8) 2¼" (5.72cm) x WOF strips

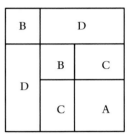

Finished Block:
15" (38.10cm) square

Pieced and Quilted by Sandy Berg
Finished Quilt Size:
Lap Size—64" x 81" (162.56 x 205.74cm)

Bonnie Scotsman Block Construction

1. Sew 3½" (8.89cm) x WOF strips of fabric A to 2½" (6.35cm) x WOF strips of fabric C, RST, to make (5) strip sets. Press the seams toward fabric C. Cut the sets into (48) 3½" (8.89cm) segments.

Make 5 strip sets, cut 48 segments

2. Sew 2½" (6.35cm) x WOF strips of fabric B to 3½" (8.89cm) x WOF strips of fabric C, RST, to make (3) strip sets. Press the seams toward fabric C. Cut the sets into (48) 2½" (6.35cm) segments.

Make 3 strip sets, cut 48 segments

3. Sew 5½" (13.97cm) x WOF strips of fabric D to 2½" (6.35cm) x WOF strips of fabric B, RST, to make (3) strip sets. Press the seams toward fabric D. Cut the sets into (48) 2½" (6.35cm) segments.

Make 3 strip sets, cut 48 segments

4. Following the diagram below, lay out the segments from steps 1-3 and the 2½" x 5½" (6.35 x 13.97cm) fabric D rectangles. Sew the segments and fabric D rectangles together as shown. Make (48) Bonnie Scotsman blocks.

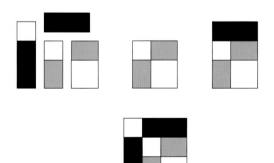

Make 48

Assembling the Blocks

1. Lay out (2) Bonnie Scotsman blocks, and a 1½" x 7½" (3.81 x 19.05cm) connector strip, making sure the fabric A squares in the blocks are positioned, as shown. Sew the blocks together with a connector strip in between. Press the seams toward the connector strips. Make (24) half blocks.

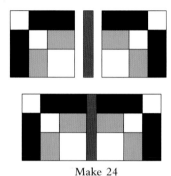

Make 24

2. Sew a connector strip to opposite ends of the 1½" (3.81cm) fabric B square and press the seams toward the connector strip. Make (12) connector strips.

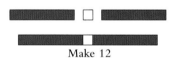

Make 12

3. Sew a completed connector strip from step 2, between (2) completed half blocks from step 1, paying attention to the position of the white A squares. Press the seams toward the connector strips. Trim the block to 15½" (39.37cm). Make (12) full blocks.

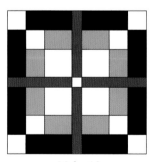

Make 12

Making Sashing Strips and Stars

1. Using Template A, page 109, trim one end of (10) 2½" x 15½" (6.35 x 39.37cm) fabric B sashing strips. Trim both ends of (7) 2½" x 15½" (6.35 x 39.37cm) fabric B sashing strips.

2. Fold a 2⅞" (7.30cm) x WOF strip of star fabric in half, WST. Using Template B, page 109, cut a set of star points. As you continue to cut points across the folded strip, rotating the template, you will create a left/right or mirrored set of points. Keeping the points separated in (2) groups, cut (24) left and right star points. Cut (24) left and right points.

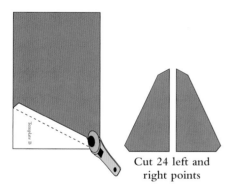

Cut 24 left and right points

3. Place a star point on the right side of the trimmed end of the sashing strip, RST. Match the raw edges of the outside tip with the trimmed edge of the sashing strip and sew with a ¼" (0.64cm) seam allowance. Press the seam open.

4. Repeat with the reverse star point and press the seam open. Trim the star points along the long edges of the strip, if necessary. Make (10) single star point sashing strips from step 1.

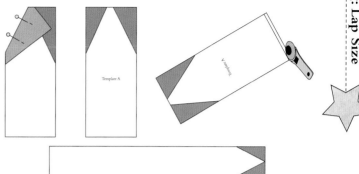

Make 10

5. Make (7) double star point sashing strips, repeating steps 1–4 for both ends.

Make 7

6. Referring to the illustration below, make sashing rows. Make (3) strips, using (2) single and (1) double star point sashing, and (2) 2½" (6.35cm) star fabric squares. Press the seams toward the sashing strips.

Make 3

7. Lay out the blocks and single star point sashing, as shown below. Sew (2) rows of (3) blocks with (2) single star point sashing strips together. Press the seams toward the sashing.

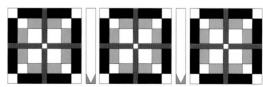

Make 2

8. Lay out blocks with double star point sashing. Sew (2) rows of (3) blocks with (2) double star point sashing strips. Press the seams toward the sashing.

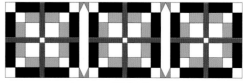

Make 2

Assembling the Quilt Center

1. Referring to the Quilt Assembly Diagram, lay out the rows and sashing strips as shown.

2. Sew the rows and strips together to finish the quilt top. Press the seams toward the sashing rows.

Adding the Borders

1. Sew (7) 2" (5.08cm) x WOF B strips together on the diagonal to make one long strip. Measure the quilt length through the center of the quilt. Cut two side border sections from the long strip, equal to the length measurement. Sew the border sections to each side of the quilt center, pressing the seams to the outside.

2. Measure the quilt width through the center of the quilt, including the side borders. From the remaining long fabric B strip, cut (2) border strips equal to the width measurement. Sew to the top and bottom of the quilt, pressing seams to the outside.

3. Sew the 4½" (11.43cm) x WOF, outer border fabric strips together on the diagonal to make one long strip. Repeat steps 1 and 2 to add outer borders to the quilt center. Press the seams to the outside.

Finishing the Quilt

1. Layer, baste, and quilt as desired.

2. Sew (8) 2¼" (5.72cm) x WOF binding fabric strips together, joining them with diagonal seams. Refer to Binding the Quilt, pages 14–17, for binding instructions.

Quilt Assembly Diagram

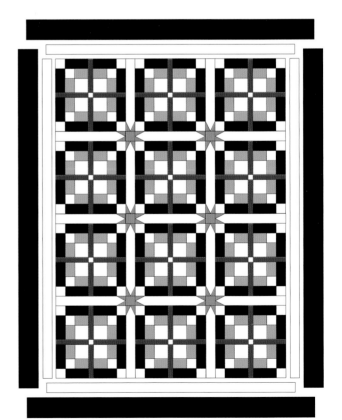

Star Crossing

Twin/Full Size

Cutting Instructions

NOTE: Keep fabric cuts organized by color and size.

From fabric A, cut:
(8) 3½" (8.89cm) x WOF strips

From fabric B, cut:
(10) 2½" (6.35cm) x WOF strips, set aside for strip sets
(16) 2½" (6.35cm) x WOF strips, from the strips, cut:
  (31) 2½" x 15½" (6.35 x39.37cm) segments:
  from the leftover 2½" (6.35cm) strip fabric, cut:
  (20) 1½" (3.81cm) block joining squares
(8) 2" (5.08cm) x WOF strips for inner borders

From fabric C, cut:
(5) 3½" (8.89cm) x WOF strips
(8) 2½" (6.35cm) x WOF strips

From fabric D, cut:
(5) 5½" (13.97cm) x WOF strips
(12) 2½" (6.35cm) x WOF strips, from the strips, cut:
  (80) 2½" x 5½" (6.35 x 13.97cm) rectangles

From the block connector fabric, cut:
(16) 1½" (3.81cm) x WOF strips, from the strips, cut:
  (80) 1½" x 7½" (3.81 x 19.05cm) rectangles

From the star fabric, cut:
(1) 2½" (6.35cm) x WOF strip, from the strip, cut:
  (12) 2½" (6.35cm) squares
(3) 2⅞" (7.30cm) Reserve this strip for star points

From outer border fabric, cut:
(10) 4½" (11.43cm) x WOF strips

From binding fabric, cut:
(10) 2¼" (5.72cm) x WOF strips

Materials

- 1 yard (91.44cm)
  light colors for fabric A
- 2¼ yards (205.74cm)
  light colors for fabric B
- 1⅛ yards (102.87cm)
  medium or dark colors
  for fabric C
- 1¾ yards (160.02cm)
  medium or dark colors
  for fabric D
- ⅜ yard (34.29cm)
  for star fabric
- 1⅓ yards (121.92cm) outer border
- ¾ yard (68.58cm)
  for block connector fabric
- 8⅞ yards (811.53cm)
  batting and backing fabric
- ¾ yard (68.58cm) for binding
- Star Point Templates (page 109)

Pieced and Quilted by Sandy Berg
Finished Quilt Size:
Twin/Full—81" x 98" (205.74 x 248.92cm)

Bonnie Scotsman Block Construction

1. Sew 3½" (8.89cm) x WOF strips of fabric A to 2½" (6.35cm) x WOF strips of fabric C, RST, to make (8) strip sets. Press the seams toward fabric C. Cut the sets into (80) 3½" (8.89cm) segments.

Make 8 strip sets, cut 80 segments

2. Sew 2½" (6.35cm) x WOF strips of fabric B to 3½" (8.89cm) x WOF strips of fabric C, RST, to make (5) strip sets. Press the seams toward fabric C. Cut the sets into (80) 2½" (6.35cm) segments.

Make 5 strip sets, cut 80 segments

3. Sew 5½" (13.97cm) x WOF strips of fabric D to 2½" (6.35cm) x WOF strips of fabric B, RST, to make (5) strip sets. Press the seams toward fabric D. Cut the sets into (80) 2½" (6.35cm) segments.

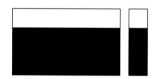

Make 5 strip sets, cut 80 segments

4. Following the diagram below, lay out the segments from steps 1-3, and the 2½" x 5½" (6.35 x 13.97cm) fabric D rectangles. Sew the segments and fabric D rectangles together as shown. Make (80) Bonnie Scotsman blocks.

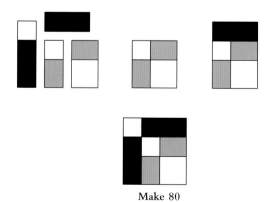

Make 80

Assembling the Blocks

1. Lay out (2) Bonnie Scotsman blocks, and a 1½" x 7½" (3.81 x 19.05cm) connector strip, making sure the fabric A squares in the blocks are positioned, as shown. Sew the blocks together with a connector strip in between. Press the seams toward the connector strips.

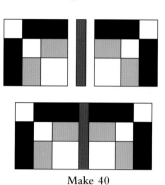
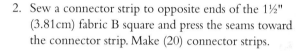

Make 40

2. Sew a connector strip to opposite ends of the 1½" (3.81cm) fabric B square and press the seams toward the connector strip. Make (20) connector strips.

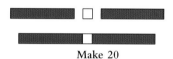

Make 20

3. Sew a completed connector strip from step 2, between (2) completed half blocks from step 1, paying attention to the position of the white, A squares. Press the seams toward the connector strips. Trim the block to 15½" (39.37cm).

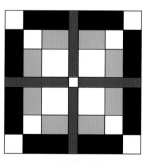

Make 20

Making Sashing Strips and Stars

1. Using Template A, page 109, trim one end of (14) 2½" x 15½" (6.35 x 39.37cm) fabric B sashing strips. Trim both ends of (17) 2½" x 15½" (6.35 x 39.37cm) fabric B sashing strips.

2. Fold a 2½" (6.35cm) x WOF strip of star fabric in half, wrong sides together. Using Template B, page 109, cut a set of star points. As you continue to cut points across the folded strip, rotating the template, you will create a left/right, or mirrored set of points. Keeping the points separated in two groups, cut (48) left and right star points.

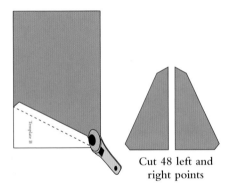

Cut 48 left and right points

3. Place a star point on the right side of the trimmed end of the sashing strip, RST. Match the raw edges of the outside tip with the trimmed edge of the sashing strip and sew with a ¼" (0.64cm) seam allowance. Press the seam open.

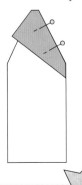

4. Repeat with the reverse star point and press the seam open. Trim the star points along the long edges of the strip, if necessary. Make (14) single star point sashing strips from step 1.

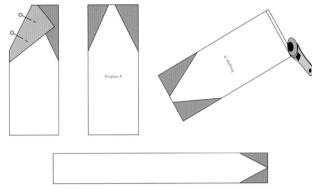

Make 14

5. Make (17) double star point sashing strips, repeating steps 1–4 for both ends.

Make 17

6. Referring to the illustration below, make sashing rows. Make (4) strips, using (2) single and (2) double star point sashing, and (3) 2½" (6.35cm) star fabric squares. Press the seams toward the sashing strips.

Make 4

7. Lay out the blocks and single star point sashing, as shown below. Sew (2) rows of (4) blocks with (3) single star point sashing strips together. Press the seams toward the sashing.

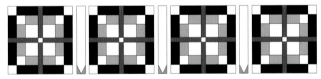

Make 2

8. Lay out blocks with double star point sashing. Sew (3) rows of (4) blocks with (3) double star point sashing strips. Press the seams toward the sashing.

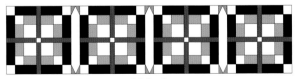

Make 3

Assembling the Quilt Center

1. Referring to the Quilt Assembly Diagram, lay out the rows and sashing strips as shown.

2. Sew the rows and strips together to finish the quilt top. Press the seams toward the sashing rows.

Adding the Borders

1. Sew (8) 2" (5.08cm) x WOF B strips together on the diagonal to make one long strip. Measure the quilt length through the center of the quilt. Cut (2) side border sections from the long strip, equal to the length measurement. Sew the border sections to each side of the quilt center, pressing the seams to the outside.

2. Measure the quilt width through the center of the quilt including the side borders. From the remaining long fabric B strip, cut (2) border strips equal to the width measurement. Sew to the top and bottom of the quilt, pressing seams to the outside.

3. Sew the 4½" (11.43cm) x WOF outer border fabric strips together on the diagonal to make one long strip. Repeat steps 1 and 2 to add outer borders to the quilt center. Press the seams to the outside.

Finishing the Quilt

1. Layer, baste, and quilt as desired.

2. Sew (10) 2¼" (5.72cm) x WOF binding fabric strips together, joining them with diagonal seams. Refer to Binding the Quilt, pages 14–17, for binding instructions.

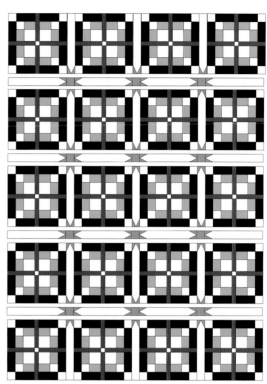

Quilt Assembly Diagram

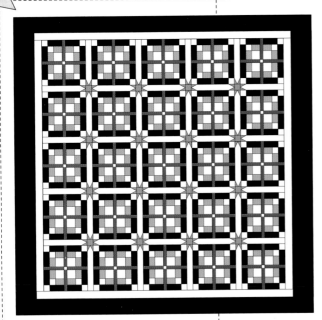

Star Crossing

Queen/King Size

Cutting Instructions

From fabric A, cut:
(10) 3½" (8.89cm) x WOF strips

From fabric B, cut:
(14) 2½" (6.35cm) x WOF strips, set aside for strip sets
(20) 2½" (6.35cm) x WOF strips, from the strips, cut:
    (40) 2½" x 15½" (6.35 x39.37cm) segments:
    from the leftover 2½" (6.35cm) strip fabric, cut:
    (25) 1½" (3.81cm) block joining squares
(10) 2" (5.08cm) x WOF strips for inner borders

From fabric C, cut:
(7) 3½" (8.89cm) x WOF strips
(10) 2½" (6.35cm) x WOF strips

From fabric D, cut:
(7) 5½" (13.97cm) x WOF strips
(15) 2½" (6.35cm) x WOF strips, from the strips, cut:
    (100) 2½" x 5½" (6.35 x 13.97cm) rectangles

From the block connector fabric, cut:
(20) 1½" (3.81cm) x WOF strips, from the strips, cut:
    (100) 1½" x 7½" (3.81 x 19.05cm) rectangles

From star fabric, cut:
(1) 2½" (6.35cm) x WOF strip, from the strip, cut:
    (16) 2½" (6.35cm) squares
(4) 2⅞" (7.30cm) strips for star points

From outer border fabric, cut:
(11) 4½" (11.43cm) x WOF strips

From binding fabric, cut:
(11) 2¼" (5.72cm) x WOF strips

Materials

- 1⅛ yards (102.87cm)
  light colors
  for fabric A

- 3 yards (274.32cm)
  light colors for fabric B

- 1¼ yards (114.3cm)
  medium or dark colors
  for fabric C

- 2¼ yards (205.74cm)
  medium or dark colors
  for fabric D

- ½ yard (45.72cm)
  for star fabric

- 1½ yards (137.16cm)
  outer border

- 1 yard (91.44cm)
  for block connector fabric

- 8⅞ yards (811.53cm)
  batting and backing fabric

- ¾ yard (68.58cm)
  for binding

- Star Point Templates (page 109)

Pieced and Quilted by Sandy Berg
Finished Quilt Size:
Queen/King—98" (248.92cm) square

Bonnie Scotsman Block Construction

1. Sew 3½" (8.89cm) x WOF strips of fabric A to 2½" (6.35cm) x WOF strips of fabric C, RST, to make (10) strip sets. Press the seams toward fabric C. Cut the sets into (100) 3½" (8.89cm) segments.

Make 10 strip sets, cut 100 segments

2. Sew 2½" (6.35cm) x WOF strips of fabric B to 3½" (8.89cm) x WOF strips of fabric C, RST, to make (7) strip sets. Press the seams toward fabric C. Cut the sets into (100) 2½" (6.35cm) segments.

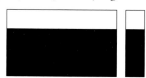

Make 7 strip sets, cut 100 segments

3. Sew 5½" (13.97cm) x WOF strips of fabric D to 2½" (6.35cm) x WOF strips of fabric B, RST, to make (7) strip sets. Press the seams toward fabric D. Cut the sets into (100) 2½" (6.35cm) segments.

Make 7 strip sets, cut 100 segments

4. Following the diagram below, lay out the segments from steps 1-3, and the 2½" x 5½" (6.35 x 13.97cm) fabric D rectangles. Sew the segments and fabric D rectangles together as shown. Make (100) Bonnie Scotsman blocks.

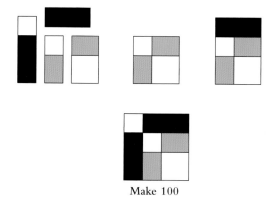

Make 100

Assembling the Blocks

1. Lay out (2) Bonnie Scotsman blocks, and a 1½" x 7½" (3.81 x 19.05cm) connector strip, making sure the fabric A squares in the blocks are positioned, as shown. Sew the blocks together with a connector strip in between. Press the seams toward the connector strips. Make (50) half blocks.

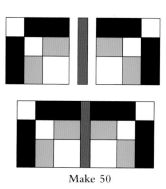

Make 50

2. Sew a connector strip to opposite ends of the 1½" (3.81cm) fabric B square and press the seams toward the connector strip. Make (25) connector strips.

Make 25

3. Sew a completed connector strip from step 2, between two completed half blocks from step 1, paying attention to the position of the white, A squares. Press the seams toward the connector strips. Trim the block to 15½" (39.37cm). Make (25) full blocks.

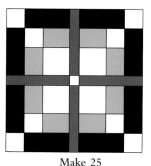

Make 25

Making Sashing Strips and Stars

1. Using Template A, page 109, trim one end of (16) 2½" x 15½" (6.35 x 39.37cm) fabric B sashing strips. Trim both ends of (24) 2½" x 15½" (6.35 x 39.37cm) fabric B sashing strips.

2. Fold a 2½" (6.35cm) x WOF strip of star fabric in half, wrong sides together. Using Template B, page 109, cut a set of star points. As you continue to cut points across the folded strip, rotating the template, you will create a left/right, or mirrored set of points. Keeping the points separated in two groups, cut (64) left and right star points.

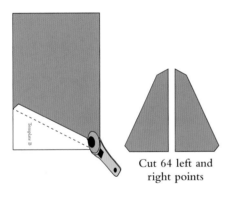

Cut 64 left and right points

3. Place a star point on the right side of the trimmed end of the sashing strip, RST. Match the raw edges of the outside tip with the trimmed edge of the sashing strip and sew with a ¼" (0.64cm) seam allowance. Press the seam open.

4. Repeat with the reverse star point and press the seam open. Trim the star points along the long edges of the strip, if necessary. Make (16) single star point sashing strips from step 1.

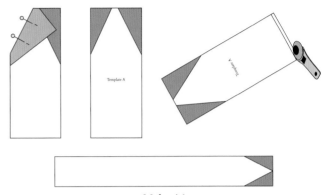

Make 16

5. Make (24) double star point sashing strips repeating steps 1–4 for both ends.

Make 24

6. Referring to the illustration below, make sashing rows. Make (4) strips using (2) single and (3) double star point sashing, and (4) 2½" (6.35cm) star fabric squares. Press the seams toward the sashing strips.

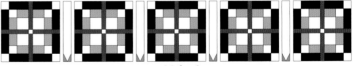

Make 4

7. Lay out the blocks and single star point sashing, as shown below. Sew (2) rows of (5) blocks with (4) single star point sashing strips together. Press the seams toward the sashing.

Make 2

8. Lay out blocks with double star point sashing. Sew (3) rows of (5) blocks with (4) double star point sashing strips. Press the seams toward the sashing.

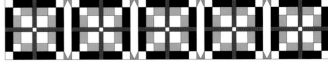

Make 3

Assembling the Quilt Center

1. Referring to the Quilt Assembly Diagram, lay out the rows and sashing strips as shown.

2. Sew the rows and strips together to finish the quilt top. Press the seams toward the sashing rows.

Adding the Borders

1. Sew (10) 2" (5.08cm) x WOF B strips together on the diagonal to make one long strip. Measure the quilt length through the center of the quilt. Cut two side border sections from the long strip, equal to the length measurement. Sew the border sections to each side of the quilt center, pressing the seams to the outside.

2. Measure the quilt width through the center of the quilt including the side borders. From the remaining long fabric B strip, cut (2) border strips equal to the width measurement. Sew to the top and bottom of the quilt, pressing seams to the outside.

3. Sew the 4½" (11.43cm) x WOF outer border fabric strips together on the diagonal to make one long strip. Repeat steps 1 and 2 to add outer borders to the quilt center. Press seams to the outside.

Finishing the Quilt

1. Layer, baste, and quilt as desired.

2. Sew (11) 2¼" (5.72cm) x WOF binding fabric strips together, joining them with diagonal seams. Refer to Binding the Quilt, pages 14–17, for binding instructions.

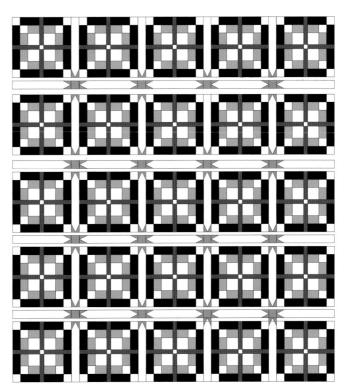

Quilt Assembly Diagram

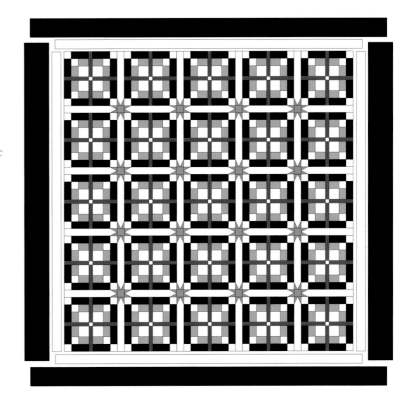

Point the Way

I asked my husband to help me find a name for this quilt. He said that when he looked at the pattern, it made him think of arrows. Sometimes you just have to go with it, so I named this one Point the Way. Once the thought was in my head, I couldn't think of anything better.

Materials

- 2¾ yards (251.46cm) light background fabric
- ½ yard (45.72cm) blue fabric
- ½ yard (45.72cm) rust fabric
- ⅛ yard (11.43cm) orange fabric
- 1 yard (91.44cm) green fabric
- 2⅛ yards (194.31cm) brown fabric
- 4⅝ yards (422.91cm) batting and backing fabric
- ⅝ yard (57.15cm) binding fabric

Cutting Instructions

From the light background fabric, cut:
(4) 6½" (16.51cm) x WOF strips, from (2) of the strips, cut:
    (8) 6½" x 9½" (16.51 x 24.13cm) rectangles, reserve the leftover strips
(2) 4" (10.16cm) x WOF strips, from the strips, cut:
    (20) 4" (10.16cm) squares
(17) 3½" (8.89cm) x WOF strips, from (2) of the strips, cut:
    (20) 3½" (8.89cm) squares
    From (13) strips, cut (20) 3½" x 15½" (8.89 x 39.37cm) strips, and
    (16) 3½" x 6½" (8.89 x 16.51cm) rectangles, reserve the leftover strips

From the blue fabric, cut:
(2) 6½" (16.51cm) x WOF strips, from the strips, cut:
    (8) 6½" (16.51cm) squares

From the rust fabric, cut:
(2) 4" (10.16cm) x WOF strips, from the strips, cut:
    (20) 4" (10.16cm) squares
(2) 3½" (8.89cm) x WOF strips, from the strips, cut:
    (20) 3½" (8.89cm) squares

From the orange fabric, cut:
(1) 3½" (8.89cm) x WOF strip, from the strip, cut:
    (5) 3½" (8.89cm) squares

From the green fabric, cut:
(8) 3½" (8.89cm) x WOF strips, from (2) of the strips, cut:
    (12) 3½" (8.89cm) squares, reserve the leftover strips

From the brown fabric, cut:
(4) 6½" (16.51cm) x WOF strips, from the strips, cut:
    (12) 6½" x 9½" (16.51 x 24.13cm) rectangles, reserve the remaining strips
(13) 3½" (8.89cm) x WOF strips, from (5) of the strips, cut:
    (10) 3½" x 15½" (8.89 x 39.37cm) strips
    From (4) strips, cut:
        (8) 3½" x 18½" (8.89 x 46.99cm) strips
    From (2) strips, cut:
        (2) 3½" x 33½" (8.89 x 85.09cm) strips, reserve the rest of the strips

From the binding fabric, cut;
(8) 2¼" (5.72cm) x WOF strips

Pieced and Quilted by Sandy Berg
Finished Quilt: 75" (190.50cm) square
Finished Block: 15" (38.10cm) square

Making Arrow Points

1. On the wrong side of (20) light background 4" (10.16cm) squares, draw a diagonal line.

2. Place a marked 4" (10.16cm) light background fabric square on top of a 4" (10.16cm) rust square, RST. Sew ¼" (0.64cm) away from both sides of the diagonal line. Cut in half on the marked line and press seam toward the rust. Trim the HSTs to 3½" (8.89cm) square. Make (40) HST units.

Make 40

3. With RST, sew a 3½" (8.89cm) light background square to the left side of (20) HSTs. The rust should be on the lower left side of the unit, as shown. Press the seams to the light background square. Make (20) units.

Make 20

4. With RST, sew a 3½" (8.89cm) rust square to the right side of (20) HSTs. The rust should be on the upper right side of the unit, as shown. Press the seams to the rust square. Make (20) units.

Make 20

5. Referring to the illustration, sew a unit from steps 3–4, RST, matching the center seams. Press the seam toward the rust arrow point. Square to 6½" (16.51cm). Make (20) arrow point units.

Make 20

Block 1

1. Sew a 3½" (8.89cm) x WOF green strip to the top of a 6½" (16.51cm) x WOF light background strip. Press the seam toward the green. Make (2) strip sets. Cut the strip sets into (16) 3½" x 9½" (8.89 x 24.13cm) segments.

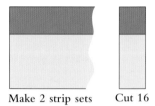

Make 2 strip sets   **Cut 16**

2. Sew a 3½" (8.89cm) x WOF light background strip to one side of a 3½" (8.89cm) x WOF green strip. Sew a 3½" (8.89cm) x WOF brown strip to the other side of the green strip. Press seams toward the green. Make (1) strip set. Cut the set into (11) 3½" x 9½" (8.89 x 24.13cm) segments. From leftover fabric, cut a 3½" (8.89cm) brown, green, and light background fabric square to make (1) segment. You need a total of (12) segments.

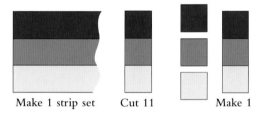

Make 1 strip set   **Cut 11**   **Make 1**

3. With RST, sew a 3½" (8.89cm) x WOF green strip on top of a 6½" (16.51cm) x WOF brown strip. Press the seam toward the green strip. Cut the strip set into (11) 3½" x 9½" (8.89 x 24.13cm) segments. From leftover fabrics, make a last segment from a 3½" x 6½" (8.89 x 16.51cm) brown rectangle and a 3½" (8.89cm) green square. You need a total of (12) segments.

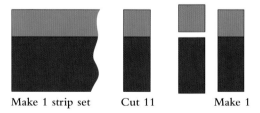

Make 1 strip set   **Cut 11**   **Make 1**

4. Sew together segments from steps 1–3, as shown in the diagram below. Press the seams toward the center.

Make 12 nine-patch blocks

5. Sew a 3½" (8.89cm) x WOF green strip to one side of a 3½" (8.89cm) x WOF light background strip, RST. Press the seam toward the green fabric. Cut the strip set into (11) 3½" x 6½" (8.89 x 16.51cm) segments. From leftover fabrics make a last segment from a 3½" (8.89cm) light background and green fabric square. You need a total of (12) segments.

Make 1 strip set Cut 11 Make 1

6. Sew a 3½" (8.89cm) x WOF green strip to one side of a 3½" (8.89cm) x WOF brown strip, RST. Press the seam toward the green fabric. Cut the strip set into (11) 3½" x 6½" (8.89 x 16.51cm) segments. From leftover fabrics create a last segment from a 3½" (8.89cm) green and brown fabric square. You need a total of (12) segments.

Make 1 strip set Cut 11 Make 1

7. Referring to the illustration, sew segments from steps 5–6 together to make four-patch segments. Press the seam toward the green and brown segment. Make (12) four-patch units. Sew a 3½" x 6½" (8.89 x 16.51cm) rectangle of light background fabric to the right side of a four-patch unit, and press the seam toward the background rectangle.

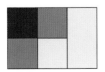

Make 12

8. Sew an arrow point to the right side of the five-patch to complete the bottom half of Block 1. Press the seam toward the arrow point. Make (12) units.

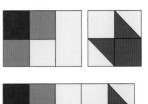

Make 12

9. Sew a 6½" x 9½" (16.51 x 24.13cm) rectangle of brown on the left side of the nine-patch from step 4 of Block 1. Press the seam toward the brown rectangle. Make (12) top half units.

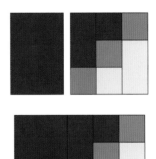

Make 12

10. Sew the top half to the bottom half to complete Block 1. Press the seam in either direction. Make (12) of Block 1.

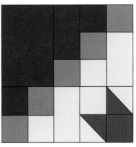

Make 12

Block 2

1. On the wrong side of (8) blue 6½" (16.51cm) squares, draw a diagonal line.

2. With RST, place a marked 6½" (16.51cm) blue square to the top of a 6½" x 9½" (16.51 x 24.13cm) light background rectangle with the drawn line running from the lower left corner of the square to the upper right corner. Sew on the drawn line. Trim the corner ¼" (0.64cm) away from the sewn line and press the seam toward the blue. Make (4) units.

Make 4 left corner units

3. With RST, place a marked 6½" (16.51cm) blue square to the top of a 6½" x 9½" (16.51 x 24.13cm) light background rectangle with the drawn line running from the upper left corner of the square to the lower right corner, sew on the drawn line. Trim the corner ¼" (0.64cm) away from the sewn line and press the seam toward the blue. Make (4) units.

Make 4 right corner units

4. With an arrow point pointing toward the lower left, sew a right corner unit to the right side of the arrow unit. Press the seams toward the right corner unit. Make (4) block 2 bottom units, measuring 6½" x 15½" (16.51 x 39.37cm).

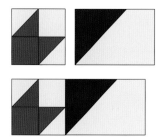

Make 4

5. With an arrow point pointing toward the upper right, sew a 3½" x 6½" (8.89 x 16.51cm) light background rectangle to the left side of the arrow point. Press the seam toward the arrow point. Make (4) units, measuring 6½" x 9½" (16.51 x 24.13cm).

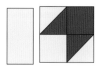

Make 4

6. Sew a 3½" x 9½" (8.89 x 24.13cm) light background/green segment from step 1 of Block 1, to the bottom of the arrow point unit from step 5. Press the seam away from the arrow unit. Make (4) units, measuring, 9½" (24.13cm) square.

Make 4

7. With an arrow point unit pointing toward the upper right, sew a left corner unit to the left of a unit from step 6. Press the seam away from the arrow unit. Make (4) top-half, Block 2 units, measuring 9½" x 15½" (24.13 x 39.37cm).

Make 4

8. Sew the top and bottom units of Block 2 together, as shown. Press the seams toward the top half. Make (4) blocks, measuring 15½" (39.37cm) square.

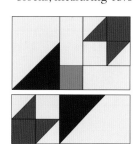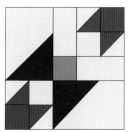

Make 4

Making Sashing Rows

1. To opposite sides of a 3½" (8.89cm) orange square, sew a 3½" x 15½" (8.89 x 39.37cm) strip of light background fabric. Press the seams toward the background. Make (5) sashing segments.

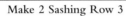

Make 5

2. Sew a green 3½" (8.89cm) square to one end of (2) of the sashing segments from step 1. Sew a green square to each end of the sashing segment and press seams toward the light background. Make (2) Sashing Row 1.

Make 2 Sashing Row 1

3. Sew a green 3½" (8.89cm) square to both ends of the remaining sashing segment. Sew a brown 3½" x 18½" (8.89 x 46.99cm) strip to the each end of the strip and press the seams toward the brown fabric.

Make 1 Sashing Row 2

4. Make (2) more sashing rows by sewing a 3½" (8.89cm) green square to both ends of a 3½" x 33½" (8.89 x 85.09cm) brown strip. Next, add a 3½" x 18½" (8.89 x 46.99cm) brown strip to both ends. Press the seams toward the brown. Make (2) Sashing Row 3.

Make 2 Sashing Row 3

Making Block Rows

1. Lay out (4) Block 1 (3) 3½" x 15½" (8.89 x 39.37cm) brown strips, and (2) 3½" x 15½" (8.89 x 39.37cm) light background strips, as shown. Sew together and press seams away from the blocks. Make (2) rows.

Make 2

2. Lay out (2) Block 1, (2) Block 2, (2) brown 3½" x 15½" (8.89 x 39.37cm) strips, and (3) light background 3½" x 15½" (8.89 x 39.37cm) strips, as shown. Sew together and press seams away from the blocks. Make (2) rows.

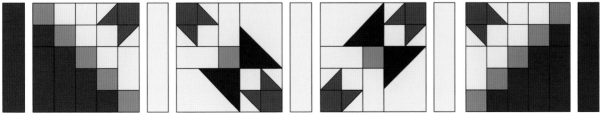

Make 2

3. Following the Quilt Assembly Diagram, lay out the rows and sashings as shown. Sew sashing and rows together, pressing the seams toward the darker fabric.

4. This is a borderless quilt. To secure and prevent the seams from opening, stay-stitch ⅛" (0.32cm) from the edges of the quilt.

Finishing the Quilt

1. Layer the backing, batting, and quilt top. Baste and quilt as desired.

2. Sew together (8) 2¼" (5.72cm) x WOF binding strips with a diagonal seam. Refer to Binding the Quilt, pages 14–17, for binding instructions.

Quilt Assembly Diagram

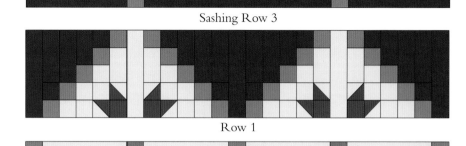

Sashing Row 3

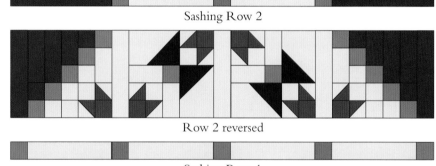

Row 1

Sashing Row 1

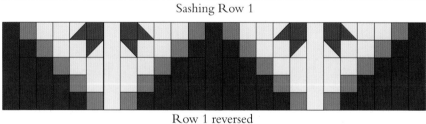

Row 2

Sashing Row 2

Row 2 reversed

Sashing Row 1

Row 1 reversed

Sashing Row 3

Starburst

Using up scraps feels so good! All those leftovers from previous projects creating another quilt—fantastic! This quilt creates star-like blocks, each featuring a different color.

Cutting Instructions

From scraps of background fabric, cut:
(78) 2½" (6.35cm) squares
(17) 2½" x 16½" (6.35 x 41.91cm) strips
(6) 3" (7.62cm) squares
(20) 3½" x 13½" (8.89 x 34.29cm) strips
(24) 4½" (11.43cm) squares
(24) 2½" x 6½" (6.35 x 16.51cm) strips
2½" (6.35cm) strips or scraps of background fabric in varying lengths, sewn end-to-end for a total of 175" (444.5cm)

From assorted print fabric, cut:
(24) 2½" x 8½" (6.35 x 21.59cm) strips
(24) 2½" x 6½" (6.35 x 16.51cm) strips
(24) 2½" x 4½" (6.35 x 11.43cm) strips
NOTE: The stars in the project quilt are coordinated, using 6 different color schemes

From dark inner border fabric, cut:
(7) 2" (5.08cm) x WOF strips

From light blue fabric, cut:
(10) 2½" (6.35cm) squares for small star centers

From blue print fabric, cut:
(1) 3" (7.62cm) x WOF strip. From the strip, cut:
     (6) 3" (7.62cm) squares
(2) 2½" (6.35cm) x WOF strips. From the strips, cut:
     (28) 2½" (6.35cm) squares
(7) 5½" (13.97cm) x WOF strips

From the binding fabric, cut:
(8) 2¼" (5.72cm) x WOF strips
     NOTE: You can piece the binding strips from scraps to total approximately 300" (762cm)

Materials

The yardage for the background and print star strips is meant to be from strips and scraps from your stash. The yardage is "approximate."

- 3 yards (274.32cm) strips and scraps of light colored background fabrics
- 1 yard (91.44cm) of assorted 2½" (6.35cm) print strips for star block
- ½ yard (45.72cm) dark fabric for inner border
- ⅛ yard (11.43cm) light blue fabric for small star centers
- 1⅓ yard (121.87cm) blue print fabric for small star points and outer border
- 5 yards (457.20cm) batting and backing fabric
- ⅝ yard (57.15cm) binding fabric

Pieced and Quilted by Sandy Berg
Finished Quilt: 62" x 80" (157.48 x 203.20cm)
Finished Block: 16" (40.64cm) square

Making the Blocks

1. Draw a diagonal line on the wrong side of (72) 2½" (6.35cm) background fabric squares.

2. Using the (24) 2½" x 4½" (6.35 x 11.43cm) print strips, align a 2½" (6.35cm) background fabric square on a print rectangle. The diagonal line on the square should go from the upper left to the lower right. Sew on the line and trim ¼" (0.64cm) from the sewn line. Open the triangle and press the seam in either direction. Make (24) left-hand pointed strips from each of the 4½" (11.43cm) and 4½" (11.43cm) print strips.

Make 24

3. Using the 2½" x 6½" (6.35 x 16.51cm) and 2½" x 8½" (6.35 x 21.59cm) print strips, align a 2½" (6.35cm) background fabric square on a strip, with the diagonal line going from the lower left to the upper right. Sew on the line and trim ¼" (0.64cm) from the sewn line. Open the triangle and press the seam in either direction. Make (24) right-hand pointed strips from the 6½" (6.35cm) and 8½" (11.43cm) print strips.

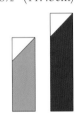

Make 24
2½" x 6½"
(6.35 x 16.51cm)

Make 24
2½" x 8½"
(6.35 x 21.59cm)

4. Sew a 4½" (11.43cm) background fabric square to one of the 2½" x 4½" (6.35 x 11.43cm) units from step 2. Press the seam toward the strip. Trim the unit to 4½" x 6½" (11.43 x 16.51cm). Make (24) units.

Make 24

5. Sew a 2½" x 6½" (6.35 x 16.51cm) strip from step 3 to the unit from step 4. Press the seam toward the strip. Trim the unit to 6½" (16.51cm) square. Make (24) units.

Make 24

6. Sew a 2½" x 6½" (6.35 x 16.51cm) background fabric strip to the top of the unit from step 5. Press the seam toward the strip. Trim the unit to 6½" x 8½" (16.51 x 21.59cm). Make (24) units.

Make 24

7. Sew a 2½" x 8½" (6.35 x 21.59cm) strip from step 3 to the left side of the unit from step 6. Press the seams toward the strip. Trim the unit to 8½" (21.59cm) square. Make (24) block units.

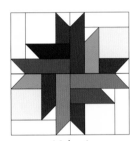

Make 24

8. Lay out (4) of the units and sew together to form the Starburst block. Make (6) and square them to 16½" (41.91cm).

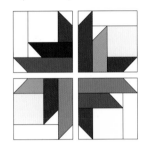

Make 6

Making the Sashing

1. Draw a diagonal line on the wrong side of (28) 2½" (6.35cm) border fabric squares.

2. On either end of a 2½" x 16½" (6.35 x 41.91cm) background fabric strip, sew a marked 2½" (6.35cm) square of blue border fabric, noting the direction of the drawn line in the illustration below. Sew on the marked line and trim ¼" (0.64cm) from the sewn line. Open the triangle and press the seam to the outside. Make (11) Sashing 1 units.

Make 11 Sashing 1 units

3. Referring to the diagram below, sew a marked 2½" (6.35cm) square to the end of a 2½" x 16½" (6.35 x 41.91cm) background fabric strip. Trim ¼" (0.64cm) from the sewn line. Open the triangle and press the seam to the outside. Make (6) Sashing 2 units.

Make 6 Sashing 2 units

4. Referring to the diagram below, sew (2) Sashing 2 strips with a 2½" (6.35cm) square of background. Press the seams away from the square. Make (2) units.

Make 2

5. Sew a 2½" (6.35cm) light blue square to each end of the strip from step 4, to complete the top and bottom sashing strips. Press the seams away from the light blue fabric square. Make (2) Sashing 3 units.

Make 2 Sashing 3 units

6. Join (2) sections of Sashing 1 units with a 2½" (6.35cm) light blue square. Then sew 2½" (6.35cm) light blue squares to the ends of the Sashing 1 units. Press the seams toward the squares in all (3) places. Make (2) Sashing 4 units.

Make 2 Sashing 4 units

Making the Quilt Center

1. Sew a Sashing 1, Starburst block, Sashing 2, Starburst block, and Sashing 1, together, as shown in the diagram, to make the top row of the quilt center. Press the seams toward the sashing strips.

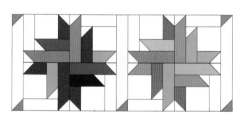

Top Row

2. Sew a Sashing 1, Starburst block, Sashing 2, Starburst block, and Sashing 1 together, as shown in the diagram, to make the bottom row of the quilt center. Pay attention to the orientation of the center sashing strip. Press the seams toward the sashing strips.

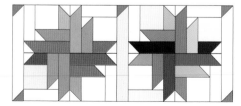

Bottom Row

3. Sew a Sashing 1, Starburst block, Sashing 1, Starburst block, and Sashing 1 together, as shown in the diagram, to make the middle row of the quilt center.

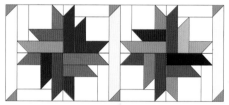

Bottom Row

4. Following the Quilt Center Diagram, sew Sashing strips 3 and 4, to the block rows and press the seams toward the sashing strips to finish the quilt center.

Quilt Center Diagram

Adding the Inner Borders

1. Draw a diagonal line on the wrong side of (6) 3" (7.62cm) background fabric squares.

2. Align a background fabric square from step 1 on top of a 3" (7.62cm) blue print border square. Sew with ¼" (0.64cm) seam on both sides of the marked line. Cut apart on the marked line. Press the seams toward the blue print. Make (12) HSTs. Trim to 2½" (6.35cm) square.

Make 12

3. From the 175" (444.5cm) background fabric strip, cut the following for inner border strips:

   For side borders, cut:
   (6) 16½" (41.91cm) strips
       For the top/bottom borders, cut:
   (2) 34½" (87.63cm)

4. Referring to the diagram below, connect (3) 16½" (41.91cm) background fabric strips from step 3, with (4) HSTs from step 2, and (2) 2½" (6.35) squares, paying attention to orientation of the HSTs. Repeat to make (2) side border strips.

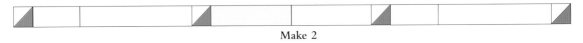

Make 2

5. Referring the diagram below, connect a 34½" (87.63cm) background fabric strip from step 3, with (2) HSTs from step 2, and (2) 2½" (6.35) background squares, paying attention to orientation of the HSTs and squares. Repeat to make (2) top and bottom border strips.

Make 2

6. Sew the side borders from step 4 to each long side of the quilt center and press the seams to the outside. Sew the top and bottom borders from step 5 to the quilt center, pressing seams to the outside.

7. Sew (5) 3½" x 13½" (8.89 x 34.29cm) background fabric rectangles together, end to end. Make (2) side border units. Center the units on the sides of the quilt center and sew, trimming the edges even with the quilt center. Press the seams to the outside of the quilt.

8. Sew (5) 3½" x 13½" (8.89 x 34.29cm) background fabric rectangles together, end to end. Make (2) top/bottom border units. Center the units on the top and bottom of the quilt center and sew, trimming the edges even with the quilt center. Press the seams to the outside of the quilt.

9. Sew (7) 2" (5.08cm) x WOF dark blue inner border strips together on the diagonal to make one long strip. Measure the quilt length through the center of the quilt. Cut two side border sections from the long strip, equal to the length measurement. Sew the border sections to each side of the quilt center, pressing the seams to the outside.

10. Measure the quilt width through the center of the quilt including the side borders. From the remaining long dark blue inner border strip, cut (2) border strips equal to the width measurement. Sew to the top and bottom of the quilt, pressing seams to the outside.

11. Use the same method with the (7) 5½" (13.97cm) x WOF blue print outer border strips to make the final borders for the quilt. Press the seams towards the outside.

Finishing the Quilt

1. Layer the backing, batting, and quilt top. Baste and quilt as desired.

2. Sew (8) 2¼" (5.72cm) x WOF strips of binding fabric with a diagonal seam to create a strip long enough to go around the outside of the quilt. Refer to Binding the Quilt, pages 14–17, for binding instructions.

Starry Night

This quilt was designed specifically to be awarded to two very special military veterans—my cousin Bob Witham, and our close family friend Bob Staal. Both of these gentlemen are Vietnam veterans whose service to the country is treasured. The blocks that go around the quilt make one mindful of award ribbons given to servicemen to honor their service. And what patriotic quilt could be without some stars? The log cabin blocks are a reminder of home. Gentlemen, thank you for your service!

Materials

- 2¾ yards (251.46cm) white background fabric
- 1¼ yards (114.3cm) red fabric for blocks and inner border
- ⅝ yard (57.15cm) gold fabric for squares and star points
- 2⅜ yards (217.17cm) dark blue fabric for blocks and borders
- ⅞ yard (80.01cm) medium blue fabric for star points
- ⅛ yard (11.43cm) light blue fabric for Log Cabin blocks
- 5¼ yards (480.06cm) batting and backing fabric
- ¾ yard (68.58cm) binding fabric
- Optional Tool: Tri-Recs Tool™ by Darlene Zimmerman and Joy Hoffman
- Star Point Templates (page 110)

Cutting Instructions

NOTE: Keep the fabric cuts separated and labeled by size.

From the background fabric, cut:
(12) 4" (10.16cm) x WOF strips, from (4) strips, cut:
    (32) 4" (10.16cm) squares. Reserve the rest of the strips.
(4) 2¼" (5.72cm) x WOF strips
(2) 2" (5.08cm) x WOF strips for log cabin blocks
(21) 1¾" (4.45cm) x WOF strips, from (6) strips, cut:
    (16) 1¾" x 11" (4.45 x 27.94cm) sashing strips, reserve the rest of the strips

From the red fabric, cut:
(6) 4" (10.16cm) x WOF strips
(1) 3" (7.62cm) x WOF strip, from the strip, cut:
    (4) 3" (7.62cm) squares
(8) 2" (5.08cm) x WOF strips for the inner border

From the gold fabric, cut:
(2) 4" (10.16cm) x WOF strips, from (1) strip, cut:
    (4) 4" (10.16cm) squares, reserve the rest of the strips
(4) 2¼" (5.72cm) x WOF strips

From the dark blue fabric, cut:
(8) 4½" (11.43cm) x WOF strips for outer borders
(6) 4" (10.16cm) x WOF strips, from (1) strip, cut:
    (4) 4" (10.06cm) squares, reserve the rest of the strips
(6) 2¼" (5.72cm) x WOF strips, from the strips, cut:
    (28) 2¼" x 7½" (6.35 x 19.05cm) strips
(3) 2" (5.08cm) x WOF strips for Log Cabin blocks

From the medium blue fabric, cut:
(5) 4" (10.16cm) x WOF strips, from (2) strips, cut:
    (12) 4" (10.06cm) squares, reserve the rest of the strips
(2) 1¾" (4.45cm) x WOF strips for Log Cabin blocks

From the light blue fabric, cut:
(1) 1¾" (4.45cm) x WOF strip for Log Cabin blocks

From the binding fabric, cut:
(9) 2¼" (5.72cm) x WOF strips

Pieced and Quilted by Alice Gwinn, Pomeroy, WA
Finished Quilt: 72½" x 85½" (184.15 x 217.17cm)
Finished Block: 10½" (26.67cm) square

Making the Strip Sets

1. Sew a 4" (10.16cm) x WOF background fabric strip to each side of a 4" (10.16cm) x WOF red fabric strip. Press the seams to the red. The strip set should measure 11" (27.94cm) x WOF. Cut the strip set into (18) 1¾" x 11" (4.45 x 27.94cm) segments.

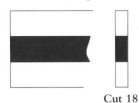

Cut 18

2. Sew a 2¼" (5.72cm) x WOF background fabric strip to each side of a 4" (10.16cm) x WOF red fabric strip. Press the seams toward the red. Make (2) strip sets measuring 7½" (19.05cm) x WOF. Cut the strip sets into (14) 4" x 7½" (10.06 x 19.05cm) segments.

Cut 14

3. Sew a 2¼" (5.72cm) x WOF gold fabric strip to each side of a 4" (10.16cm) x WOF background fabric strip. Press the seams toward the gold. Make (2) strip sets measuring 7½" (19.05cm) x WOF. Cut the strip sets into (28) 2¼" x 7½" (10.06 x 19.05cm) segments.

Cut 28

4. Sew a 4" (10.16cm) x WOF dark blue fabric strip to each side of a 4" (10.16cm) x WOF red fabric strip. Press the seams toward the dark blue. Make (2) strip sets measuring 11" (27.94cm) x WOF. Cut the strip sets into (28) 2¼" (5.72cm) segments.

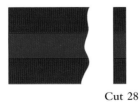

Cut 28

Making Puss in the Corner Blocks

1. Sew a gold strip segment to each side of a red strip segment. Press the seams towards the center. Square up the block to 7½" (19.05cm). Make (14) blocks.

Make 14

2. On the back of the Puss in the Corner block, you will see two sets of seams pressed toward the corner squares. On these (2) sides, sew a 2¼" x 7½" (10.06 x 19.05cm) dark blue fabric strip and press these seams toward the outside of the block. Make (14) units, paying attention to the direction of the seams.

Make 14

3. Sew a dark blue/red segment , to the remaining two sides of the units from step 2. Press the seams towards the outside. The units should measure 11" (27.94cm) square. Make (14) blocks.

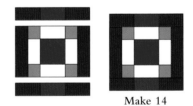

Make 14

Making the Stars

NOTE: This pattern includes templates (page 110) to make the star points for the stars in the center of the quilt. Refer to pages 8–10, Making Elongated Star Points, for instructions.

1. Layer (2) 4" (10.16cm) x WOF gold fabric strips, RST. Using Template A, page 110, make (16) and (16) reversed gold star points.

Make 16 and 16 reversed

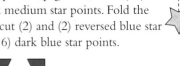

2. Using (3) 4" (10.16cm) x WOF background fabric strips and Template B, follow the step-by-step instructions, pages 8–10 to make (40) background star triangles.

Make 40

3. Place a gold star point and a gold reverse star point from step 1, on either side of a background star triangle to form a square. Layer one of the star points on top of the triangle, aligning the edges, and sew with a scant ¼" (0.64cm) seam. Press the seam open. Repeat with the second star point. Square the units to 4" (10.16cm). Make (8) units.

Make 8

4. Using a 4" (10.16cm) x WOF red fabric strip and Template B, page 110, make (8) red star triangles. Place a gold star point and a gold reverse star point from step 1 of this section, on either side of a red star triangle to form a square. Layer one of the star points on top of the triangle, aligning the edges, and sew with a scant ¼" (0.64cm) seam. Press the seam open. Repeat with the second star point. Square the units to 4" (10.16cm). Make (8) units.

Make 8

5. Lay out the following units to form a nine-patch star, as shown:
   • (3) 4" (10.16cm) background squares
   • (1) 4" (10.16cm) dark blue square
   • (2) background/gold star point blocks
   • (2) red/gold star point blocks
   • (1) 4" (10.16cm) gold square

Sew the units together in rows and sew the rows together to make a corner star. Press the seams open to reduce bulk. Make (4) 11" (27.94cm) corner star blocks.

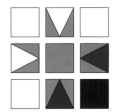

Make 4

6. Layer (2) 4" (10.16cm) x WOF dark medium fabric strips, RST. Using template A, page 110, make (14) and (14) reversed dark medium star points. Fold the third strip in half and cut (2) and (2) reversed blue star points, for a total of (16) dark blue star points.

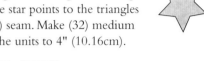

Make 16 and 16 reversed

7. With the remaining background triangles from step 2 of this section, sew blue star points to the triangles with a scant ¼" (0.64cm) seam. Make (32) medium blue star points. Square the units to 4" (10.16cm).

Make 32

8. Lay out the following units to form a nine-patch star, as shown:
   • (4) 4" (10.16cm) background squares
   • (4) background/medium blue star points
   • (1) 4" (10.16cm) medium blue square

Sew the units together in rows and sew the rows together to make a center star. Press the seams open to reduce bulk. Make (8) 11" (27.94cm) center star blocks.

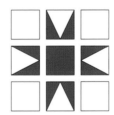

Make 8

Making the Log Cabin Blocks

1. With RST, sew a 1¾" x 3" (4.45 x 7.62cm) background fabric strip to one side of a 3" (7.62cm) red square. Press the seam toward the background fabric. Make (4) Log Cabin centers.

Make 4

2. Turn the center one turn to the right. On the right side of the center, sew (1) 1¾" x 4¼" (4.45 x 10.80cm) background fabric strip. Press the seam toward the background fabric. Continue turning the unit one turn to the right, and cut and add the following strips to the right side after each turn.
   • 1¾" x 4¼" (4.45 x 10.80cm) light blue
   • 1¾" x 5½" (4.45 x 13.97cm) light blue. Square up to 5½" (13.97cm) to complete Round 1 of the block.
   • 1¾" x 5½" (4.45 x 13.97cm) background
   • 1¾" x 6¾" (4.45 x 17.15cm) background
   • 1¾" x 6¾" (4.45 x 17.15cm) medium blue
   • 1¾" x 8" (4.45 x 20.32cm) medium blue. Square up to 8" (20.32cm) to complete Round 2.
   NOTE the change in width in the following strips:
   • 2" x 8" (5.08 x 20.32cm) background
   • 2" x 9½" (5.08 x 24.13cm) background
   • 2" x 9½" (5.08 x 24.13cm) dark blue
   • 2" x 11" (5.08 x 27.94cm) dark blue. Square up to 11" (27.94cm) to complete the block.

   Square the block to 11" (27.94cm). Make (4) Log Cabin blocks.

Make 4

Assembling the Quilt Center

1. Following the order in the illustration, lay out (2) corner stars, (3) Puss in the Corner blocks, and (4) background/red sashing strips from step1, page 72. Sew the row, using a ¼" (0.64cm) seam allowance. Press the seams toward the sashing. Make (2) rows, one for the top and one for the bottom of the quilt center.

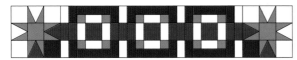

Make 2

2. Following the order in the illustration, lay out (2) Puss in the Corner blocks, (2) Log Cabin blocks, a center star block, and (4) 1¾" x 11" (4.45 x 27.94cm) background fabric sashing strips. Sew the row, using a ¼" (0.64cm) seam allowance. Press the seams toward the sashing. Make (2) rows, one for row 2, and one for row 5 of the quilt center.

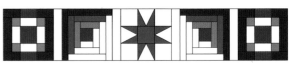

Make 2

3. Following the order in the illustration, sew (1) Puss in the Corner block, (3) blue center star blocks, and (1) Puss in the Corner block. Sew a 1¾" x 11" (4.45 x 27.94cm) background fabric sashing strip between each of the blocks. Press the seams toward the sashing. Make (2) rows, one each for rows 3 and 4.

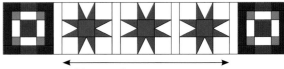

Make 2

4. Measure the distance between the seams of the (2) outside Puss in the Corner blocks blocks from step 2, as shown. It should measure approximately 36¾" (93.35cm). Add ½" (1.27cm) to the measurement for seam allowance.

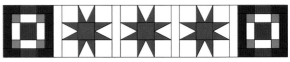

Measure from seam to seam

5. Using the measurement from step 4, and using the (5) 1¾" (4.45cm) x WOF reserved strips of background fabric, cut (5) sashing rows to go between the rows of the quilt. Sew a 1¾" x 11" (4.45 x 27.94cm) segment from step 1, page 72, to each end of the (5) strips. Press the seams towards the sashing.

Make 5

6. Lay out the rows and sashing rows as shown in the Quilt Center Assembly Diagram. Sew the rows and sashing rows together and press the seams toward the sashing rows.

Adding the Borders

1. Sew the (8) 2" (5.08cm) x WOF red inner border strips together on the diagonal. Measure the quilt length through the center of the quilt. Cut (2) side border sections from the long strip, equal to the length measurement. Sew the border sections to each side of the quilt center, pressing the seams to the outside.

2. Measure the quilt width through the center of the quilt including the side borders. From the remaining long fabric strip, cut (2) red inner border strips equal to the width measurement. Sew to the top and bottom of the quilt, pressing seams to the outside.

3. Use the same method with the (8) 4½" (11.43cm) x WOF dark blue outer border strips to make the final borders for the quilt. Press the seams towards the outside.

Finishing the Quilt

1. Layer the backing, batting, and quilt top. Baste and quilt as desired.

2. Sew (9) 2¼" (5.72cm) x WOF binding fabric strips together, joining them with diagonal seams. Refer to Binding the Quilt, pages 14–17, for binding instructions.

Quilt Center Assembly Diagram

Window on the Stars

Reminiscent of a marble tile floor or a stained glass window, the border of this quilt gives it an "Arts and Crafts" or "Art Deco" flair.

Materials

- 2 yards (182.88cm) background fabric
- ⅓ yard (30.48cm) dark purple fabric
- ¼ yard (22.86cm) medium purple fabric
- ⅓ yard (30.48cm) light purple fabric
- ¾ yard (68.58cm) dark green fabric
- 1⅛ yards (102.87cm) medium green fabric
- ⅞ yard (80.01cm) yellow/green fabric
- 4½ yards (411.48cm) batting and backing fabric
- ½ yard (45.72cm) binding fabric

Cutting Instructions

From the background fabric, cut:
(2) 5½" (13.97cm) x WOF strips, from the strips, cut:
  (12) 5½" (13.97cm) squares
(6) 5" (12.7cm) x WOF strips, from the strips, cut:
  (4) 5" (12.7cm) squares
  (14) 5" x 12½" (12.7 x 31.75cm) rectangles
(6) 4½" (11.43cm) x WOF strips, from the strips, cut:
  (48) 4½" (11.43cm) squares

From the dark green fabric, cut:
(2) 5½" (13.97cm) x WOF strips, from the strips, cut:
  (12) 5½" (13.97cm) squares
(9) 1½" (3.81cm) x WOF strips

From medium green fabric, cut:
(7) 5" (12.7cm) x WOF strips, from the strips, cut:
  (12) 5" (12.7cm) squares
  (14) 5" x 12½" (12.7 x 31.75cm) rectangles
  (6) 4½" (11.43cm) squares

From the yellow/green fabric, cut:
(1) 4½" (11.43cm) x WOF strip, from the strip, cut:
  (6) 4½" (11.43cm) squares
(15) 1½" (3.81cm) x WOF strips

From the dark purple fabric, cut:
(2) 5½" (13.97cm) x WOF strips, from the strips, cut:
  (12) 5½" (13.97cm) squares

From the medium purple fabric, cut:
(2) 2½" (6.35cm) x WOF strips, from the strips, cut:
  (24) 2½" (6.35cm) squares

From the light purple fabric, cut:
(2) 5½" (13.97cm) x WOF strips, from the strips, cut:
  (12) 5½" (13.97cm) squares

From the binding fabric, cut:
(7) 2¼" (5.72cm) X WOF strips

Pieced by Sharon Ledbetter, Clarkston, WA
Quilted by Kate Pippen, Vancouver, WA (*pippenquilting.com*)
Finished Quilt: 60" x 72" (152.4 x 182.88cm)
Finished Block: 12" (30.48cm) square

Making the Stars

1. Draw a diagonal line on the back of:
   - (12) 5½" (13.97cm) dark green squares,
   - (24) 2½" (6.35cm) medium purple squares, and
   - (12) 5½" (13.97cm) light purple squares.

2. Align a 5½" (13.97cm) dark green and background fabric square, RST. Sew ¼" (0.64cm) away on both sides of the drawn line. Cut on the line and press the seams toward the dark green fabric. Repeat to make (12) HSTs.

Make 12

3. Cut the HSTs from step 2, in half across the seam to make (24) small triangle units.

Make 24

4. Layer a marked 5½" (13.97cm) dark green square on top of a 5½" (13.97cm) dark purple square, RST. Sew ¼" (0.64cm) away on both sides of the drawn line. Cut on the line and press the seams toward the dark green fabric. Repeat to make (12) HSTs.

Make 12

5. Cut the HSTs from step 4, in half across the seam to make (24) small triangle units.

Make 24

6. Align a small triangle unit from steps 3 and 5 along the long, cut edge, RST. Sew and press the seams in either direction. Make (24) quarter-square triangles (QST). Square to 4½" (11.43cm).

Make 24

7. Align a marked 2½" (6.35cm) medium purple square on one corner of a 4½" (11.43cm) background square. Sew on the marked line and trim ¼" (0.64cm) away from the sewn line. Open the triangle and press the seam toward the triangle. Repeat to make (24) corner squares. They should measure 4½" (11.43cm).

Make 24

8. Lay out (4) dark purple/dark green QST units, (4) corner squares, and (1) 4½" (11.43cm) yellow/green square, as shown. Sew into (3) rows of (3) units. In the middle row, press the seams toward the center square. In the top and bottom rows, press the seams to the outside. Sew the (3) rows together and press the seams toward the outside. They should measure 12½" (31.75cm) square. Make (6) #1 star blocks.

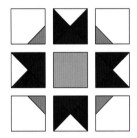 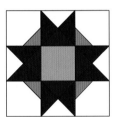

Make 6 star #1 blocks

9. Align a 5½" (13.97cm) light purple square on top of a 5½" (13.97cm) background fabric square, RST. Sew ¼" (0.64cm) away on both sides of the drawn line. Cut on the line and press the seams towards the light purple fabric. Repeat to make (12) HSTs.

Make 12

10. Cut the HSTs from step 9, in half across the seam to make (24) small triangle units.

Make 24

11. Align a 5½" (13.97cm) light purple square on top of a dark purple square, RST. Sew ¼" (0.64cm) away on both sides of the drawn line. Cut on the line and press the seams towards the light purple fabric. Repeat to make (12) HSTs.

Make 12

12. Cut the HSTs from step 11, in half across the seam to make (24) small triangle units..

Make 24

13. Align small triangle unit from steps 10 and 12 along the long cut edge, RST. Sew and press the seams in either direction. Make (24) quarter-square triangles (QST). Square to 4½" (11.43cm).

Make 24

14. Lay out (4) light/dark purple QST units, (4) 4½" (11.43cm) background squares, and (1) 4½" (11.43cm) medium green square, as shown. Sew into (3) rows of (3) units. In the middle row, press the seams toward the center square. In the top and bottom rows, press the seams to the outside. Sew the (3) rows together and press the seams toward the outside. They should measure 12½" (31.75cm). Make (6) #2 star blocks.

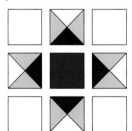

Make 6
star #2 blocks

Making Border Blocks

1. Sew a yellow/green 1½" (3.81cm) x WOF strip on each side of a dark green 1½" (3.81cm) x WOF strip to make a strip set. Press the seams open. The strip set should measure 3½" (8.89cm) x WOF. Make (7) strip sets. Cut the strip sets to make the following:
   • (14) 12½" (31.75cm) segments
   • (16) 5" (12.70cm) segments
   • (4) 1½" (3.81cm) segments

Make 7

2. Sew a dark green 1½" (3.81cm) x WOF strip to each side of a yellow/green 1½" (3.81cm) x WOF strip make a strip set. Press the seams open and cut into (8) 1½" (3.81cm) segments.

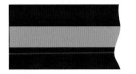

Cut 8

3. Using 1½" (3.81cm) segments from steps 1–2, make (4) nine-patch units as shown below. To reduce bulk, press seams open.

Make 4

4. Sew a 5" x 12½" (12.70 x 31.75cm) medium green rectangle and a 5" x 12½" (12.70 x 31.75cm) background rectangle to each side of a 12½" (31.75cm) strip set segment from step 1, as shown. Press the seams open. Make (14) border blocks. The blocks should measure 12½" (31.75cm) square.

Make 14 border blocks

5. Lay out (4) 5" (12.70cm) green segments from step 1, (1) nine-patch, (3) 5" (12.70cm) medium green squares, and (1) 5" (12.70cm) square of background, as shown. Sew into (3) rows of (3) units. Press the seams open. Sew the rows together, and press the seams open. Make (4) corner blocks.

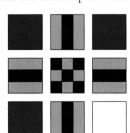

Make 4 corner blocks

Assembling the Quilt Top

1. Referring to the Quilt Assembly diagram, lay out the blocks, as shown. Sew the blocks together in rows. Press the seams open, or alternate the direction of the seams to reduce bulk. Sew the rows together to complete the quilt top.

2. Carefully sew around the edges of the quilt top, ⅛" (0.32cm) from the edge, using a little larger stitch length than normal. This will help keep seams from opening before the quilt is quilted.

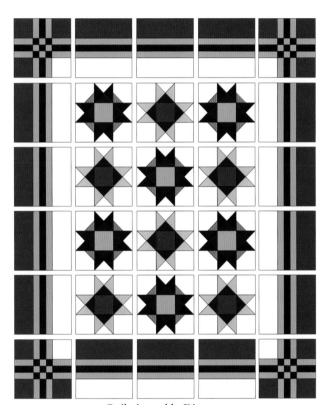

Quilt Assembly Diagram

Finishing the Quilt

1. Layer the backing, batting, and quilt top. Baste and quilt as desired.

2. Sew (7) 2¼" (5.72cm) x WOF binding fabric strips together, joining them with diagonal seams. Refer to Binding the Quilt, pages 14–17, for binding instructions.

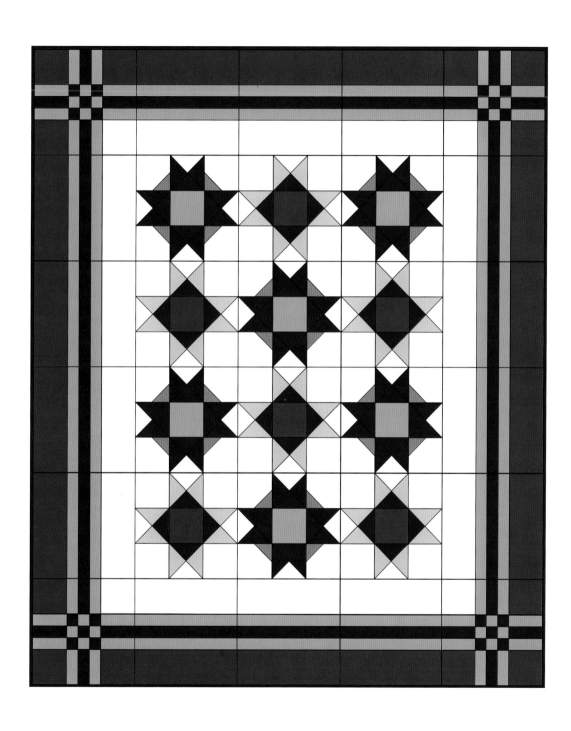

Salute to Service

The Twin Star block gives great movement to this quilt. Add the zigzag shape in the border and you have an exciting, unique pattern.

Materials

- 3½ yards (320.04cm) background fabric
- ¼ yard (22.86cm) red fabric
- ⅝ yard (57.15cm) red/white print fabric
- 1 yard (91.44cm) dark blue fabric
- ⅓ yard (30.48cm) medium blue fabric
- ¼ yard (22.86cm) light blue fabric
- 4⅓ yards (396.21cm) batting and backing fabric
- ⅝ yard (57.15cm) binding fabric

Cutting Instructions

From the background fabric, cut:
(4) 5½" (13.97cm) x WOF strips, from the strips, cut:
 (26) 5½" (13.97cm) squares, cut (2) of the squares, diagonally twice, to make (8) triangles, you will only use (7) triangles
(3) 5" (12.7cm) x WOF strips
(6) 4½" (11.43cm) x WOF strips, from (3) strips, cut:
 (24) 4½" (11.43cm) squares, reserve the rest of the strips
(10) 3½" (8.89cm) x WOF strips
(4) 3" (7.62cm) x WOF strips, from the strips, cut:
 (48) 3" (7.62cm) squares
(4) 2½" (6.35cm) x WOF strips

From the red fabric, cut:
(1) 4½" (11.43cm) x WOF strip

From the red/white print fabric, cut:
(1) 5½" (13.97cm) x WOF strip. From the strips, cut:
 (5) 5½" (13.97cm) squares, cut each square, diagonally twice, to make (20) triangles, you will only use (17) triangles
(2) 4½" (11.43cm) x WOF strips
(2) 2½" (6.35cm) x WOF strips

From the dark blue fabric, cut:
(6) 5½" (13.97cm) x WOF strips, from the strips, cut:
 (30) 5½" (13.97cm) squares, cut (6) of the squares diagonally twice to make (24) triangles

From the medium blue fabric, cut:
(2) 5" (12.7cm) x WOF strips, from the strips, cut:
 (12) 5" (12.7cm) squares, cut each square diagonally to make (24) triangles

From the light blue fabric, cut:
(1) 4½" (11.43cm) x WOF strip, from the strip, cut:
(6) 4½" (11.43cm) squares

From the binding fabric, cut:
(8) 2¼" (5.72cm) x WOF strips

Pieced and Quilted by Sandy Berg
Finished Quilt: 60¾" x 70" (154.31 x 177.8cm)
Finished Block: 12" (30.48cm) square

Making the Strip Sets

1. Sew a 2½" (6.35cm) x WOF background fabric strip to each side of a 4½" (11.43cm) x WOF red/white print strip. Press the seams toward the print. Cut (12) 2½" (6.35cm) segments.

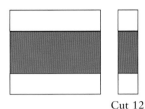

Cut 12

2. Sew a 2½" (6.35cm) x WOF background fabric strip to each side of a 4½" (11.43cm) x WOF red strip. Press the seams toward the red fabric. Cut (6) 4½" (11.43cm) segments.

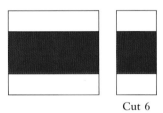

Cut 6

3. Sew a 2½" (6.35cm) x WOF red/white print fabric strip to each side of a 4½" (11.43cm) x WOF background fabric strip. Press the seams toward the print fabric. Cut (12) 2½" (6.35cm) segments.

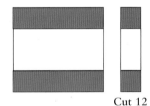

Cut 12

4. Sew a 4½" (11.43cm) x WOF background fabric strip to each side of a 4½" (11.43cm) x WOF red/white print strip. Press the seams toward the background fabric. Cut (12) 2½" (6.35cm) segments.

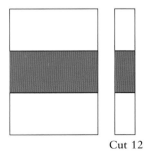

Cut 12

Making Banded Puss in the Corner Blocks

1. Referring the illustration, sew a segment from step 3 to each side of a segment from step 2. Press the seams toward the center.

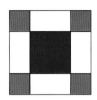

2. On the back of the Puss in the Corner block, you will see (2) sets of seams pressed toward the corner squares. On these (2) sides, sew (1) 2½" (6.35cm) red print/background segment, from step 1, and press the seams toward the outside of the block. Make (6) units, paying attention to the direction of the seams.

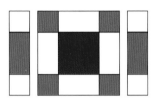

Make 6

3. To the remaining two sides of the units from step 2, add a 4½" (11.43cm) red print/background fabric segment from step 4. Press the seams toward the outside. The units should measure 12" (30.48cm) square. Make (6) banded Puss in the Corner blocks.

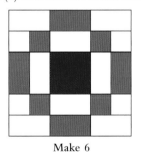

Make 6

Making the Stars

1. Using (17) red/white print triangles and (17) dark blue triangles, sew them together along a short side to make a larger triangle, as shown. Press the seams toward the dark blue.

2. Repeat step 1, using (7) background triangles and the remaining (7) dark blue triangles.

3. To these triangle units, sew a medium blue triangle to the long side of the triangles. Press the seams toward the medium blue. Square the star points to 4½" (11.43cm). Make (17) squares with the red/white point triangles at the top and (7) squares with the background triangle at the top.

Make 17   Make 7

4. Lay out the following units to make a nine-patch star, as shown:
   • (2) red/blue star points
   • (2) blue/white star points
   • (1) light blue square
   • (4) 4½" (11.43cm) background fabric squares

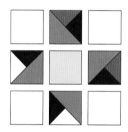

5. Sew the units together in rows. Press the seams in the top and bottom rows toward the outside. Press the seams in the middle row to the center. Sew the rows together, pressing these seams to the center. Square to 12½" (31.75cm). Make (2) blocks.

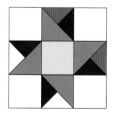

Make 2

6. Paying attention to the star point orientation, make (1) of each of the stars shown below. Sew and press the seams, referring to step 5.

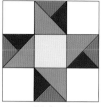

Make 3   Make 1

Assembling the Quilt Center

1. Lay out the star blocks and Banded Puss in the Corner Blocks as shown below, paying attention to the block orientation. Press the seams away from the star blocks.

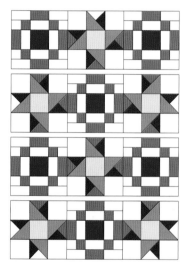

2. Sew the rows together to finish the quit center. Press the seams in either direction.

Adding Inner Borders

1. Measure the quilt from top to bottom through the center. Sew (3) 5" (12.7cm) x WOF background strips together, end-to-end, to make (2) strips equal to the measurement of the quilt. Sew a strip to each side of the quilt center. Press the seams toward the outside.

2. Measure the quilt from side to side, through the center. Sew (3) 3½" (8.89cm) x WOF background strips together, end-to-end, to make (2) strips equal to the measurement of the quilt. Sew a strip to the top and bottom of the quilt and press the seams toward the outside.

Making Pieced Borders

1. Draw a diagonal line on the wrong side of (48) 3" (7.62cm) and (24) 5½" (13.97cm) background squares.

2. Place a marked 5½" (13.97cm) background square on top of a 5½" (13.97cm) dark blue square, RST. Sew ¼" (0.64cm) away from both sides of the diagonal line. Cut in half on the marked line and press seams open to reduce bulk. The squares are oversized; square them to 5" (12.7cm). Make a total of (48) HSTs.

Make 48

3. Lay a marked 3" (7.62cm) background fabric square on the dark blue corner of an HST from step 2. Sew on the marked line and trim ¼" (0.64cm) from the sewn line. Open the triangle and press the seams open to reduce bulk. Make (48) units.

Make 48

4. Sew 44 of the units from step 3 together in pairs. Set aside the remaining 4 units. Pay attention to the orientation of the of the units. Press the seams open. The units should measure 5" x 9½" (12.7 x 24.13cm).

5. Sew (6) of the pairs together from step 4 to complete a pieced side border. Make (2) side borders. Orient the pieced border sections, following the Quilt Assembly Diagram. Sew them in place and press the seams open to reduce bulk.

Make 2

6. Sew (5) pairs together from step 4, to make a pieced border. Make a top and bottom border. Sew one of the leftover units from step 4 on each end of the top and bottom rows. Press the seams open to reduce bulk.

7. Sew the top and bottom borders to the quilt center. Press the seams open.

Quilt Assembly Diagram

Adding Outside Borders

1. Sew (7) 3½" (8.89cm) x WOF background strips together on the diagonal. Measure the quilt length through the center of the quilt. Cut (2) side border sections from the long strip, equal to the length measurement. Sew the border sections to each side of the quilt center, pressing the seams to the outside.

2. Measure the quilt width through the center of the quilt including the side borders. From the remaining long fabric strip, cut (2) outer border strips equal to the width measurement. Sew to the top and bottom of the quilt, pressing seams to the outside.

Finishing the Quilt

1. Layer the backing, batting, and quilt top. Baste and quilt as desired.

2. Sew (8) 2¼" (5.72cm) x WOF binding fabric strips together, joining them with diagonal seams. Refer to Binding the Quilt, pages 14–17, for binding instructions.

Fandango Dance

The Weathervane block is the basis for this colorful quilt. It is joined by an alternate block that frames the Weathervane block with squares of diagonal color. Dresden blocks in the corners provide a fun touch that gives this quilt its name—Fandango!

Materials

- 2⅛ yards (194.31cm) background fabric
- 1 yard (91.44cm) white fabric
- 1 yard (91.44cm) orange fabric
- ¾ yard (68.58cm) rust fabric
- ⅓ yard (30.48cm) gold fabric
- ⅝ yard (57.15cm) pale green fabric
- ⅝ yard (57.15cm) light green fabric
- ½ yard (45.72cm) medium gray/green fabric
- ½ yard (45.72cm) dark gray/green fabric
- ⅜ yard (34.29cm) medium turquoise fabric
- ¾ yard (68.58cm) medium/dark turquoise fabric
- 1¾ yards (160.02cm) border fabric
- 5⅞ yards (537.21cm) batting and backing fabric
- ⅝ yard (57.15cm) binding fabric
- Dresden Fan Template, page 111

Cutting Instructions

From the background fabric, cut:
- (5) 3" (7.62cm) x WOF strips, from the strips, cut:
  (56) 3" (7.62cm) squares
- (24) 2½" (6.35cm) x WOF strips, from the strips, cut:
  (52) 2½" x 4½" (6.35 x 11.43cm) rectangles
  (272) 2½" (6.35cm) squares

From the white fabric, cut:
- (2) 12½" (31.75cm) x WOF strips, from the strips, cut:
  (4)12½" (31.75cm) squares
  (8) 6½" (16.51cm) squares
- (3) 2½" (6.35cm) x WOF strips, from the strips, cut:
  (16) 2½" x 4½" (6.35 x 11.43cm) rectangles
  (16) 2½" (6.35cm) squares

From the gold fabric, cut:
- (2) 4½" (11.43cm) x WOF strips, from the strips, cut:
  (14) 4½" (11.43cm) squares

From the orange fabric, cut:
- (7) 4½" (11.43cm) x WOF strips, from the strips, cut:
  (56) 4½" (11.43cm) squares

From the rust fabric, cut:
- (5) 3" (7.62cm) x WOF strips, from the strips, cut:
  (56) 3" (7.62cm) squares
- (4) 2½" (6.35cm) x WOF strips, from the strips, cut:
  (56) 2½" (6.35cm) squares

From the pale green fabric, cut:
- (7) 2½" (6.35cm) x WOF strips, from the strips, cut:
  (56) 2½" x 4½" (6.35 x 11.43cm) rectangles

From the light green fabric, cut:
- (7) 2½" (6.35cm) x WOF strips, from the strips, cut:
  (104) 2½" (6.35cm) squares

From the medium gray/green fabric, cut:
- (6) 2½" (6.35cm) x WOF strips, from the strips, cut:
  (90) 2½" (6.35cm) squares

From the dark gray/green fabric, cut:
- (6) 2½" (6.35cm) x WOF strips, from the strips, cut:
  (90) 2½" (6.35cm) squares

From the medium turquoise fabric, cut:
- (8) fan blades

From the dark turquoise fabric, cut:
- (12) fan blades

From the border fabric, cut:
- (9) 6½" (16.51cm) x WOF strips

From the binding fabric, cut:
- (9) 2¼" (5.72cm) x WOF strips

Pieced and Quilted by Sandy Berg
Finished Quilt: 72" x 96" (182.88 x 243.84cm)
Finished Block: 12" (30.48cm) square

Making Weathervane Blocks

1. Draw a diagonal line on the wrong side of:
   - (112) 2½" (6.35cm) background squares
   - (56) 3" (7.62cm) background squares.

2. Layer a 2½" (6.35cm) marked background square on the upper-right corner of a 4½" (11.43cm) orange fabric square, (RST). Sew on the drawn line and trim ¼" (0.64cm) away from the sewn line. Open the triangle and press the seam toward the background fabric.

Make 56

3. Layer a 2½" (6.35cm) marked background square on the upper-left corner of unit from step 2. Sew on the drawn line and trim ¼" (0.64cm) away from the sewn line. Open the triangle and press the seam toward the background fabric. Make (56) point units.

Make 56

4. Layer a 3" (7.62cm) marked background square on top of a 3" (7.62cm) rust square, RST. Sew ¼" (0.64cm) on both sides of the drawn line. Cut on the drawn line. Press the seam toward the rust fabric. Trim to 2½" (6.35cm). Make (56) HSTs.

Make 56

5. Lay out a 2½" (6.35cm) background and rust square, and (2) HSTs from step 4, as shown. Sew into rows and press the seams toward the 2½" (6.35cm) squares. Sew the rows together and press this seam toward the side of the block with the most rust fabric. Make (56) 4½" (11.43cm) Weathervane corners.

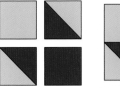

Make 56

6. Lay out (1) 4½" (11.43cm) gold square, (4) point units from step 3, and (4) Weathervane corners, as shown. Sew the units into rows and press the seams in the top and bottom rows toward the outside. In the middle row, press the seams toward the center square. Make (14) 12½" (31.75cm) Weathervane blocks.

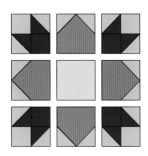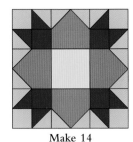

Make 14

Making Alternate Blocks

1. Draw a diagonal line on the wrong side of (52) background and (52) light green 2½" (6.35cm) squares.

2. Layer a marked 2½" (6.35cm) light green square on top of a 2½" x 4½" (6.35 x 11.43cm) background rectangle, RST, with the marked line running from the upper left to the lower right corner of the square. Sew on the line and trim the corner, leaving a ¼" (0.64cm) seam allowance. Open the triangle and press the seam toward the corner. Make (26) dark units.

Make 26 dark, right units

3. Layer a marked 2½" (6.35cm) light green square on top of a 2½" x 4½" (6.35 x 11.43cm) background rectangle, RST, with the marked line running from the lower left to the upper right corner of the square. Sew on the line and trim the corner, leaving a ¼" (0.64cm) seam allowance. Open the triangle and press the seam toward the corner. Make (26) units.

Make 26 dark, left units

4. Lay out (2) 2½" (6.35cm) light green squares and (2) 2½" (6.35cm) dark gray/green squares, as shown. Sew into rows, pressing the seams toward the dark squares. Sew the (2) rows together. Make (22) 4½" (11.43cm) dark four-patches.

Make 22 dark

5. Lay out (2) 2½" (6.35cm) background squares and (2) 2½" (6.35cm) medium gray/green squares, as shown. Sew into rows, pressing the seams toward the medium gray/green squares. Sew the (2) rows together. Make (22) 4½" (11.43cm) light four-patches.

Make 22 light

6. To complete the darker section of the alternate block, lay out (1) 2½" (6.35cm) dark gray/green square, (1) dark right strip, (1) dark left strip, and the dark four-patch, as shown. Make (22) 6½" (16.51cm) A blocks.

Make 22 A blocks

7. Layer a marked 2½" (6.35cm) background square on top of a 2½" x 4½" (6.35 x 11.43cm) pale green rectangle, RST, with the marked line running from the upper left to the lower right corner of the square.

Sew on the line and trim the corner, leaving a ¼" (0.64cm) seam allowance. Open the triangle and press the seam toward the corner. Make (26) light units.

Make 26 light, right units

8. Layer a marked 2½" (6.35cm) background square on top of a 2½" x 4½" (6.35 x 11.43cm) pale green rectangle, RST, with the marked line running from lower left to the upper right corner of the square. Sew on the line and trim the corner, leaving a ¼" (0.64cm) seam allowance. Open the triangle and press the seam toward the corner. Make (26) units.

Make 26 light, left units

9. To complete the lighter section of the alternate block, lay out (1) 2½" (6.35cm) medium gray/green square, (1) light right strip, (1) light left strip, and the light four-patch, as shown. Make (22) 6½" (16.51cm) B blocks.

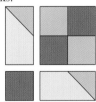

Make 22 B blocks

10. Lay out (2) of each of the A blocks and B blocks with RST, as shown. Sew the rows together RST, pressing the seams in either direction. Make (9) 12½" (31.75cm) Alternate Blocks.

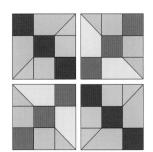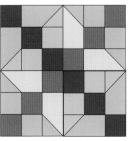

Make 9

11. Lay out a dark gray/green 2½" (6.35cm) square, a white 2½" (6.35cm) square, and a 2½" x 4½" (6.35 x 11.43cm) white rectangle, as shown. Sew together and press the seams toward the dark fabric. Make (8) units.

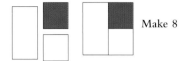

Make 8

12. Lay out (1) dark right strip from step 2, (2) 2½" (6.35cm) dark gray/green squares, (1) 2½" (6.35cm) light green square, and (1) unit from step 11, as shown. Sew the (2) side segments together, and press the seam toward the dark square. Sew the (2) top squares together, pressing the seam toward the dark square. Sew this unit to the top of square unit, then sew the side segment to the unit to complete a C block.

Make 4 C blocks

13. To make a mirrored C block, lay out (1) dark left strip, (2) 2½" (6.35cm) dark gray/green squares, (1) 2½" (6.35cm) light green square, and (1) unit from step 11, as shown. Repeat the sewing/pressing instructions in step 12 to make (4) mirrored C blocks.

Make 4 mirrored C blocks

14. Lay out (1) B block, (1) C block, (1) mirrored C block, and (1) 6½" (16.51cm) white square, as shown. Sew into rows. Press the seams to the B block in the top row and toward the white square in the bottom row. Sew the (2) rows together and press the seam toward the row with the white square. Make (4) 12½" (31.75cm) dark alternate partial blocks.

B

C mirrored

C

Make 4

15. Lay out a medium gray/green 2½" (6.35cm) square, (1) white 2½" (6.35cm) square, and (1) 2½" x 4½" (6.35 x 11.43cm) white rectangle, as shown. Sew together and press the seams toward the dark fabric. Make (8) units.

Make 8

16. Lay out (1) light left strip from step 7, (2) 2½" (6.35cm) medium gray/green squares, (1) 2½" (6.35cm) background square, and (1) unit from step 15, as shown. Sew the two top segments together, and press the seam toward the darker square. Sew the (2) side squares together, pressing the seam toward the darker square. Sew this unit to the side of square unit, then sew the top segment to the unit to make (4) 6½" (16.51cm) D blocks.

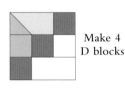

Make 4 D blocks

17. To make a mirrored D block, lay out (1) light right strip, (2) 2½" (6.35cm) medium gray/green squares, (1) 2½" (6.35cm) background square, and (1) unit from step 16, as shown. Repeat the sewing/pressing instructions in step 16 to make (4) 6½" (16.51cm) mirrored D blocks.

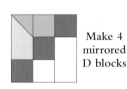

Make 4 mirrored D blocks

18. Lay out (1) A block, (1) D block, a mirrored D block, and (1) 6½" (16.51cm) white square, as shown. Sew into rows. Press the seams toward the A block in the top row and toward the white square in the bottom row. Sew the (2) rows together and press the seam toward the row with the white square. Make (4) 12½" (31.75cm) light alternate partial blocks.

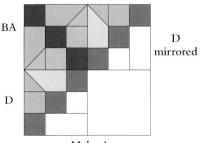

BA

D mirrored

D

Make 4

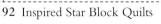

Making Dresden Blocks

1. Lay out (3) medium/dark turquoise and (2) medium turquoise Dresden Fan blades, alternating the colors, starting and ending with the medium/dark turquoise. Sew the pieces together along the long side, stopping about ¼" (0.64cm) from the start of the curve. Press the seams open. Make (4) Dresden fans.

Make 4

2. Lay a completed fan onto the corner of a 12½" (31.75cm) white fabric square, matching the edges of the fan with the edges of the square. Baste the fan shapes to the white square. On the curved edges, turn under approximately ¼" (0.64cm) and use an appliqué stitch to secure the curved edges. Make (4) 12½" (31.75cm) Dresden Fan blocks.

Make 4

Assembling the Rows

1. Lay out (2) Dresden Fan blocks, (1) Weathervane block, (1) light alternate partial block, and (1) dark alternate partial block, as shown. Sew the blocks together, pressing the seams to the right in the top row and to the left in the bottom row.

Top Row

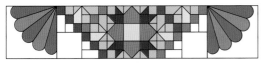

Bottom Row

2. For rows 2 and 6, lay out (2) Weathervane blocks, (1) light alternate partial block, (1) dark alternate partial block, and (1) alternate block, as shown. Press row 2 seams to the left, and the seams of row 6 to the right.

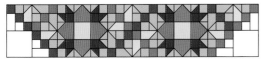

Make 2

3. For rows 3 and 5, lay out (3) Weathervane blocks and (2) Alternate blocks, as shown. Press seams to the right in both of these rows.

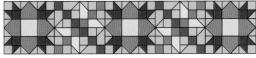

Make 2

4. For row 4, lay out (2) Weathervane blocks and (3) alternate blocks, as shown. Press the seams to the left in this row.

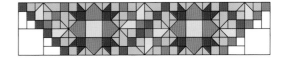

5. Following the Quilt Assembly Diagram, shown below, sew the rows together to complete the quilt top.

Quilt Assembly Diagram

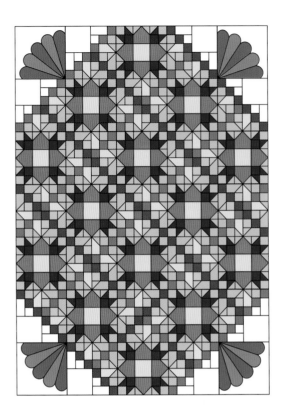

Adding the Borders

1. Sew the 6½" (16.51cm) x WOF border strips together, joining them with diagonal seams. Measure the quilt length through the center of the quilt. Cut (2) side border sections from the long strip, equal to the length measurement. Sew the border sections to each side of the quilt center, pressing seams to the outside.

2. Measure the quilt width through the center of the quilt, including the side borders. Cut (2) border strips equal to the width measurement. Sew to the top and bottom of the quilt pressing seams to the outside.

Finishing the Quilt

1. Layer, baste, and quilt as desired.

2. Sew (9) 2¼" (5.72cm) x WOF black border strips together, joining them with diagonal seams. Refer to Binding the Quilt, pages 14–17, for binding instructions.

In Honor

With its stars and stripes, this quilt is reminiscent of our national flag, also known as the "Stars and Stripes." The quilt just begs for red, white and blue!

Materials

- 3⅛ yards (34.29cm) background fabric
- ¾ yard (68.58cm) dark blue fabric
- 1¼ yards (114.3cm) medium blue fabric
- ¾ yard (68.58cm) red fabric
- 5 yards (457.20cm) batting and backing fabric
- ⅝ yard (57.15cm) binding fabric

Cutting Instructions

From the background fabric, cut:
(4) 6½" (16.51cm) x WOF strips, from the strips, cut:
    (4) 6½" x 21½" (16.51 x 54.61cm) rectangles
    (12) 3½" (8.89cm) squares
(19) 3½" (8.89cm) x WOF, from (5) strips, cut:
    (6) 3½" x 12½" (8.89 x 31.75cm) rectangles
    (18) 3½" x 6½" (8.89 x 16.51cm) rectangles
(7) 2" (5.08cm) x WOF strips for the inner border

From the dark blue fabric, cut:
(7) 3½" (8.89cm) x WOF strips

From the medium blue fabric, cut:
(1) 6½" (16.51cm) x WOF strip, from the strip, cut:
    (3) 6½" (16.51cm) squares
(10) 3½" (8.89cm) x WOF strips, from (2) strips, cut:
    (24) 3½" (8.89cm) squares, reserve the rest of the strips for the outer border

From the red fabric, cut:
(7) 3½" (8.89cm) x WOF strips

From the binding fabric, cut:
(9) 2¼" (5.72cm) x WOF strips

Pieced and Quilted by Sandy Berg
Finished Quilt: 69" x 81" (175.26 x 205.74cm)
Finished Star Block: 12" (30.48cm) square

Making the Stars

1. Draw a diagonal line on the wrong side of (24) 3½" (8.89cm) medium blue squares.

2. Layer a 3½" (8.89cm) marked medium blue square on the right side of a 3½" x 6½" (8.89 x 16.51cm) background rectangle, RST. Sew on the line and trim the corner, leaving a ¼" (0.64cm) seam allowance. Press the medium blue triangle away from the background fabric.

3. Layer a 3½" (8.89cm) marked medium blue square on the left-hand side of the unit, RST. (NOTE: This square will overlap the first square in the middle.) Sew on the marked line and trim the corner, leaving a ¼" (0.64cm) seam allowance. Press the medium blue triangle away from the background fabric to make a star point unit. Make (12) 3½" x 6½" (8.89 x 16.51cm) star point units.

Make 12

4. Sew a star point unit to opposite sides of a 6½" (16.51cm) medium blue fabric square. Press the seams toward the center square. Make (3) 6½" x 12½" (16.51 x 31.75cm) star centers.

Make 3

5. Sew a 3½" (8.89cm) background square to opposite ends of a star point unit from step 3. Press the seams towards the star point unit. Make (6) 3½" x 12½" (8.89 x 31.75cm) star top/bottom rows.

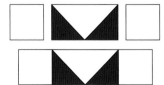

Make 6

6. Sew a star top and bottom row to a star center, as shown. Press the seams toward the center. Make (3) 12½" (31.75cm) center stars.

Make 3

7. Sew a 3½" x 12½" (8.89 x 31.75cm) background fabric rectangle to the top and bottom of each of the center stars. Press the seams toward the background fabric rectangle. Make (3) 12½" x 18½" (31.75 x 46.99cm) star units.

Make 3

Making the Strips

1. Sew a 3½" (8.89cm) x WOF background fabric strip to a 3½" (8.89cm) x WOF red fabric strip, RST. Press the seams toward the red fabric. Make (7) strip sets.

Make 7

From (4) background/red strip sets, cut one of each:
- 39½" (100.33cm)
- 36½" (92.71cm)
- 33½" (85.09cm)
- 30½" (77.47cm)

From (3) background/red strip sets, cut one of each:
- 27½" (69.85cm) and 12½" (31.75cm)
- 24½" (62.23cm) and 15½" (39.37cm)
- 21½" (54.61cm) and 18½" (46.99cm)

2. Sew a 3½" (8.89cm) x WOF background fabric strip to a 3½" (8.89cm) x WOF dark blue strip, RST. Press the seams toward the dark blue fabric. Make (7) strip sets.

Make 7

From (4) background/dark blue strip sets, cut:
- 39½" (100.33cm)
- 36½" (92.71cm)
- 33½" (85.09cm)
- 30½" (77.47cm)

From (3) background/dark blue strip sets, cut one of each:
- 27½" (69.85cm) and 12½" (31.75cm)
- 24½" (62.23cm) and 15½" (39.37cm)
- 21½" (54.61cm) and 18½" (46.99cm)

3. Sew a 3½" x 6½" (8.89 x 16.51cm) background rectangle to the right side of the strip sets listed below, keeping the red fabric at the bottom of the strip set. Press the seams toward the background rectangle.
    - 33½" (85.09cm)
    - 24½" (62.23cm)
    - 15½" (39.37cm)

4. Sew a red/background strip set to the bottom of the sets from step 3, referring to the diagram and list below. Press the seam allowance toward the strip set with the background rectangle.

    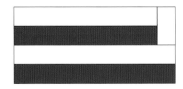

    - Sew the 36½" (92.71cm) strip to the 33½" (85.09cm)
    - Sew the 27½" (69.85cm) strip to the 24½" (62.23cm)
    - Sew the 18½" (46.99cm) strip to the 15½" (39.37cm)

5. Sew a 3½" x 6½" (8.89 x 16.51cm) background rectangle to the left side of the dark blue strip sets listed below, keeping the dark blue fabric at the top of the strip set. Press the seams toward the background rectangle.
    - 33½" (85.09cm)
    - 24½" (62.23cm)
    - 15½" (39.37cm)

6. Sew a dark blue/background strip set from step 5 to the bottom of the strip sets, referring to diagram and list below. Press the seam allowance toward the strip set with the background rectangle.

    - Sew the 36½" (92.71cm) strip to the 33½" (85.09cm)
    - Sew the 27½" (69.85cm) strip to the 24½" (62.23cm)
    - Sew the 18½" (46.99cm) strip to the 15½" (39.37cm)

7. Sew a 6½" x 21½" (16.51 x 54.61cm) background fabric rectangle between a 12½" (31.75cm) red/background strip and a 39½" (100.33cm) dark blue/background strip, as shown. Press the seams toward the background rectangle.

8. Sew a 6½" x 21½" (16.51 x 54.61cm) background fabric rectangle between a 21½" (54.61cm) red/background strip and a 30½" (77.47cm) dark blue/background strip, as shown. Press the seams toward the background rectangle.

9. Sew a 6½" x 21½" (16.51 x 54.61cm) background fabric rectangle between a 30½" (77.47cm) red/background strip and a 21½" (54.61cm) dark blue/background strip, as shown. Press the seams toward the background rectangle.

10. Sew a 6½" x 21½" (16.51 x 54.61cm) background fabric rectangle between a 39½" (100.33cm) red/background strip and a 12½" (31.75cm) dark blue/background strip, as shown. Press the seams toward the background rectangle.

Assembling the Quilt Center

1. Lay out the units as shown, paying attention to the position of the color strips. Sew to make (3) star strips. Press the seams toward the star center.

2. Following the Quilt Center Assembly Diagram, sew the long units together in the order shown. Press the seams in either direction.

Adding the Borders

1. Sew the 2" (5.08cm) x WOF background strips together, joining them with diagonal seams. Measure the quilt length through the center of the quilt. Cut (2) side border sections from the long strip, equal to the length measurement. Sew the border sections to each side of the quilt center, pressing seams to the outside.

2. Measure the quilt width through the center of the quilt including the side borders. Cut (2) border strips equal to the width measurement. Sew to the top and bottom of the quilt, pressing seams to the outside.

3. Sew the 3½" (8.89cm) x WOF medium blue strips together, joining them on the diagonal. Repeat steps 1 and 2 to add outer borders to the quilt center.

Finishing the Quilt

1. Layer, baste, and quilt as desired.

2. Sew (9) 2¼" (5.72cm) x WOF binding strips together, joining them with diagonal seams. Refer to Binding the Quilt, pages 14–17, for binding instructions.

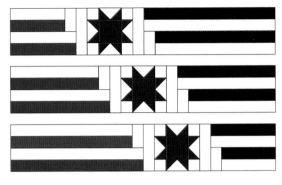

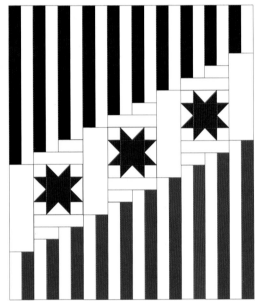

Quilt Center Assembly Diagram

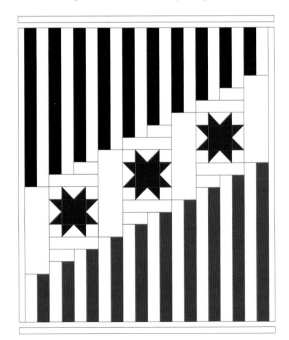

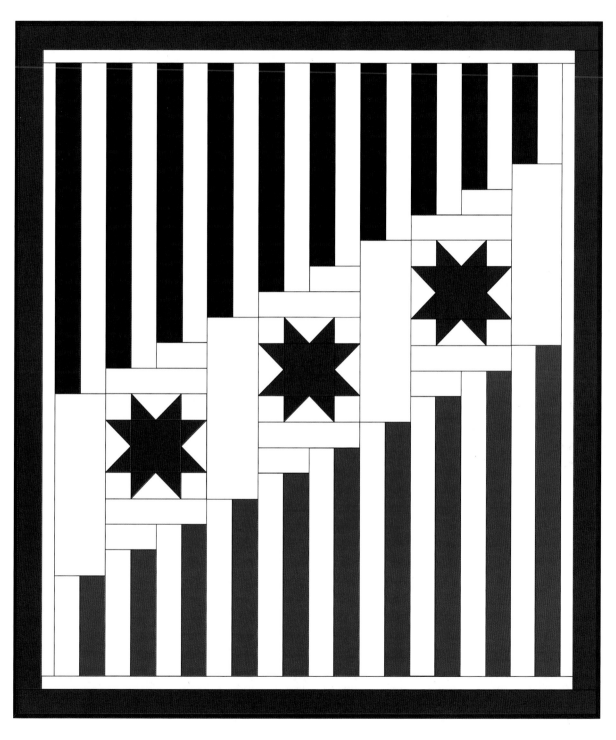

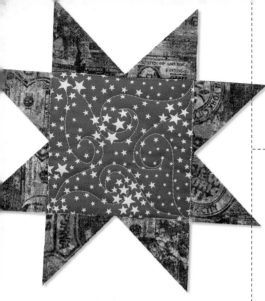

Stars of the Show

Pinwheels and stars surrounded by stripes make this a fun quilt for any star lover.

Materials

- 2⅛ yards (194.31cm) blue background fabric
- 1 yard (91.44cm) white fabric
- 1⅓ yards (121.92cm) dark blue fabric
- ¾ yard (68.58cm) medium blue fabric
- ¾ yard (68.58cm) red fabric
- ¼ yard (22.86cm) print fabric for pinwheels
- 5 yards (457.20cm) batting and backing fabric
- ⅝ yard (57.15cm) binding fabric

Cutting Instructions

From the blue background fabric, cut:
- (8) 6½" (16.51cm) x WOF strips, from (1) strip, cut:
  - (4) 6½" x 8½" (16.51 x 21.59cm) rectangles, reserve the rest of the strips
- (1) 4½" (11.43cm) x WOF strip, from the strip, cut:
  - (8) 4½" (11.43cm) squares, cut each square, twice, diagonally to make a total of (32) small triangles.
- (2) 4¼" (10.80cm) x WOF strips, from the strip, cut:
  - (16) 4¼" (10.80cm) squares, cut each square diagonally to make a total of (32) large triangles.
- (2) 2½" (6.35cm) x WOF strips, from the strips, cut:
  - (10) 2½" x 6½" (6.35 x 16.51cm) rectangles

From the white fabric, cut:
- (5) 3¼" (8.26cm) x WOF strips, from the strips, cut:
  - (24) 3¼" x 5" (8.26 x 12.7cm) rectangles
  - (24) 3¼" (8.26cm) squares
- (7) 1½" (3.81cm) x WOF strips

From the dark blue fabric, cut:
- (8) 4½" (11.43cm) x WOF strips
- (4) 2¾" (6.99cm) x WOF strips, from the strips, cut:
  - (48) 2¾" (6.99cm) squares

From the medium blue fabric, cut:
- (10) 2½" (6.35cm) x WOF strips

From the red fabric, cut:
- (1) 5" (12.7cm) x WOF strip, from the strip, cut:
  - (6) 5" (12.7cm) squares
- (7) 2½" (6.35cm) x WOF strips, from (3) strips, cut:
  - (4) 2½" x 10½" (6.35cm x 26.67cm) rectangles
  - (10) 2½" x 6½" (6.35 x 16.51cm) rectangles, reserve the rest of the strips

From the print fabric, cut:
- (1) 4½" (11.43cm) x WOF strip, from the strip, cut:
  - (8) 4½" (11.43cm) squares, cut each square, twice, diagonally to make a total of (32) small triangles

From the binding fabric, cut:
- (8) 2¼" (5.72cm) x WOF strips

Pieced and Quilted by Sandy Berg
Finished Quilt: 60" x 80" (152.40 x 203.20cm)
Finished Block: 10" (25.40cm) square

Making the Stars

1. Draw a diagonal line on the wrong side of (48) 2¾" (6.99cm) dark blue fabric squares.

2. Layer a 2¾" (6.99cm) dark blue square on the right-hand side of a 3¼" x 5" (8.26 x 12.7cm) white fabric rectangle, RST, as shown. Sew on the line and trim the corner, leaving a ¼" (0.64cm) seam allowance. Press the dark blue triangle away from the white fabric. Make (24) rectangle units.

Make 24

3. Layer a 2¾" (6.99cm) dark blue square on the left-hand side of a the white rectangle unit, RST. (NOTE: This square will overlap the first square in the middle.) Sew on the line and trim the corner, leaving a ¼" (0.64cm) seam allowance. Press the dark blue triangle away from the white fabric. Make (24) 3¼" x 5" (8.26 x 12.7cm) star point units.

Make 24

4. Sew a 3¼" (8.26cm) white fabric square to each side of a star point. Press the seams toward the white squares. Make (12) 3¼" x 10½" (8.26 x 26.67cm) star top/bottom units.

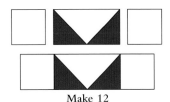

Make 12

5. Sew a star point unit to opposite sides of a 5" (12.7cm) red fabric square. Press the seams toward the red square. Make (6) 5" x 10½" (12.7 x 26.67cm) star centers.

Make 6

6. Sew a star top and bottom to the unit from step 5 to complete the star block. Press the seams to the outside. Make (6) 10½" (26.67cm) square units.

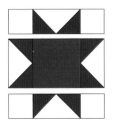 

Make 6

Making Strip Sets

1. Sew a 2½" (6.35cm) x WOF medium blue strip to the top and bottom of a 6½" (16.51cm) x WOF background fabric strip. Press the seams toward the medium blue. Make (3) strip sets.

Make 3

2. From the strip sets, cut (7) 10½" (26.67cm) squares, and (4) 2½" x 10½" (6.35cm x 26.67cm) segments. Re-press the seams of the (4) segments toward the background fabric.

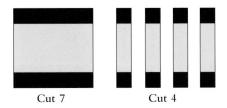

Cut 7   **Cut 4**

3. Sew a 2½" (6.35cm) x WOF medium blue strip and a 2½" (6.35cm) x WOF red strip to the top and bottom of a 6½" (16.51cm) x WOF background fabric strip. Press the seams away from the blue background. Make (4) strip sets.

Make 4

4. From the strip sets, cut (10) 10½" (26.67cm) squares, and (16) 2½" x 10½" (6.35cm x 26.67cm) segments. Re-press the seams of the (16) segments toward the background fabric.

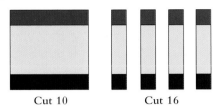

Cut 10 **Cut 16**

Making the Pinwheels

1. Layer a small triangle cut from the 4½" (11.43cm) background fabric squares, with a small print triangle of the same size. Place the background fabric on top of the print fabric, RST. Sew together on the short right side, with a ¼" (0.64cm) seam. Press the seams towards the print fabric. Make (32) partial blade units.

Make 32

2. Layer a large, blue background triangle on top of a partial blade, RST, and sew on the long side using a ¼" (0.64cm) seam allowance. Press the seams toward the blue background triangle and trim to 3½" (8.89cm) squares. Make (32).

Make 32

3. Lay out (2) pinwheel blades side by side as shown, and sew RST with a ¼" (0.64cm) seam. Press the seam toward the blue background triangle. Make (16) 3½" x 6½" (8.89 x 16.51cm) half-pinwheels.

Make 16

4. Sew 2 half-pinwheels together to form the pinwheel, as shown. Press the seam allowance in either direction. Make (8) 6½" (16.51cm) pinwheel blocks.

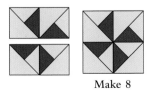

Make 8

5. Sew a 2½" x 6½" (6.35 x 16.51cm) background fabric strip to opposite sides of (2) Pinwheel blocks. Press the seams away from the pinwheel. Make (2) units.

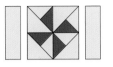

Make 2

6. Sew (1) 2½" x 10½" (6.35cm x 26.67cm) background/medium blue strip set segment to the top and bottom of a pinwheel unit, as shown. Make (2) 10½" (26.67cm) pinwheel squares.

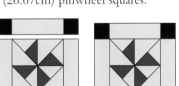

Make 2

7. On the remaining 6 Pinwheel blocks, sew (1) 2½" x 6½" (6.35cm x 16.51cm) background fabric and red fabric strip on opposite sides of the blocks, as shown. Press the seams away from the Pinwheel block. Make (6) units.

Make 6

8. Sew a 2½" x 10½" (6.35cm x 26.67cm) medium blue/red strip set segment to the top and bottom of the unit from step 7. Press the seams away from the Pinwheel block. Make (6) 10½" (26.67cm) units.

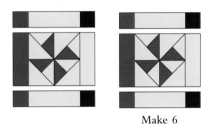

Make 6

Making the Blocks

1. Layer a 2½" x 6½" (6.35 x 16.51cm) red fabric strip on the left side of a 6½" x 8½" (16.51 x 21.59cm) background rectangle, RST. Sew together and press the seams toward the red fabric. Sew a 2½" x 10½" (6.35cm x 26.67cm) red fabric strip to the bottom of this unit. Press the seam toward the background fabric.

2. Sew a 2½" x 10½" (6.35cm x 26.67cm) medium blue/red strip set segment to the top of the unit from step 1. Press the seams away from the strip set. Make (4) corner blocks.

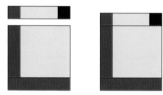

Make 4

Assembling the Rows

1. Lay out (2) red and blue strip blocks, (2) star blocks, and (1) blue strip block, as shown. Sew the units together with a ¼" (0.64cm) seam allowance and press the seams toward the red and blue strip blocks. Make (3) star rows.

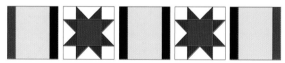

Make 3

2. Lay out (2) corner blocks, (2) red and blue strip blocks, and (1) Pinwheel block, as shown. Sew the units together with a ¼" (0.64cm) seam allowance and press the seams toward the red and blue strip blocks. Make (2) top and bottom pinwheel rows.

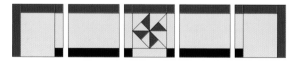

Make 2

3. Lay out (3) Pinwheel blocks and (2) blue strip blocks, as shown. Complete (2) pinwheel rows. Press each seam away from the Pinwheels. Make (2) rows.

Make 2

Adding the Borders

1. Sew the 1½" (3.81cm) x WOF white background strips together, joining them with diagonal seams. Measure the quilt length through the center of the quilt. Cut (2) side border sections from the long strip, equal to the length measurement. Sew the border sections to each side of the quilt center, pressing seams to the outside.

2. Measure the quilt width through the center of the quilt including the side borders. Cut (2) white border strips equal to the width measurement. Sew to the top and bottom of the quilt, pressing seams to the outside.

3. Sew the 4½" (11.43cm) x WOF dark blue strips together, joining them on the diagonal. Repeat steps 1 and 2 to add outer borders to the quilt center. Press the seams to the outside.

Finishing the Quilt

1. Layer, baste, and quilt as desired.

2. Sew (8) 2¼" (5.72cm) x WOF black border strips together, joining them with diagonal seams. Refer to Binding the Quilt, pages 14–17, for binding instructions.

Templates

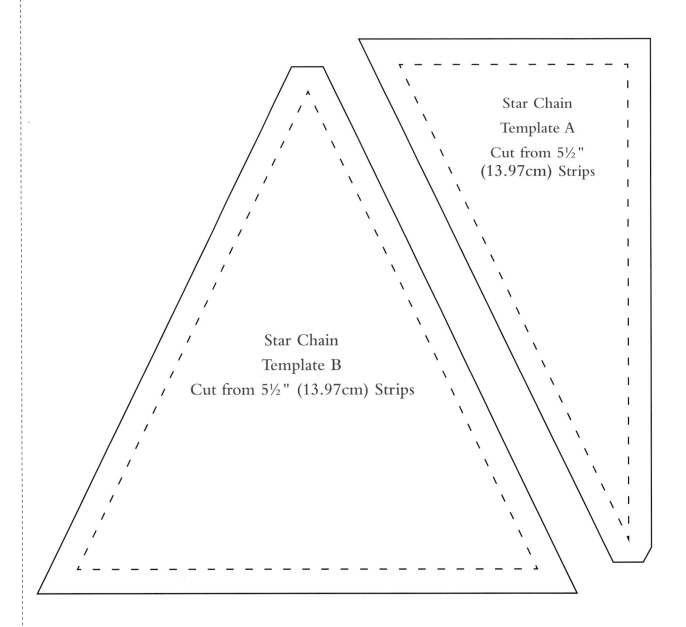

Star Chain

Template A

Cut from 5½"
(13.97cm) Strips

Star Chain

Template B

Cut from 5½" (13.97cm) Strips

Use this end to cut the
edges of the sashing strip
for the Star Points.

Star Crossing

Template A

Use with 2⅞" (7.30cm) Strips

Star Crossing
Template B
Use with 2⅞" (7.30cm) Strips

Use this end to square up the Star
Points with the sides of the sashings.

Templates

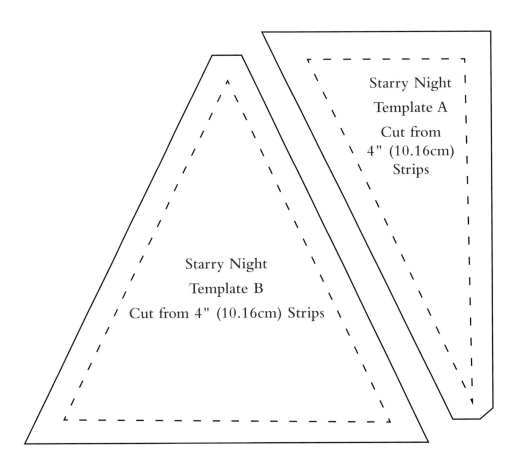

Starry Night
Template A
Cut from
4" (10.16cm)
Strips

Starry Night
Template B
Cut from 4" (10.16cm) Strips

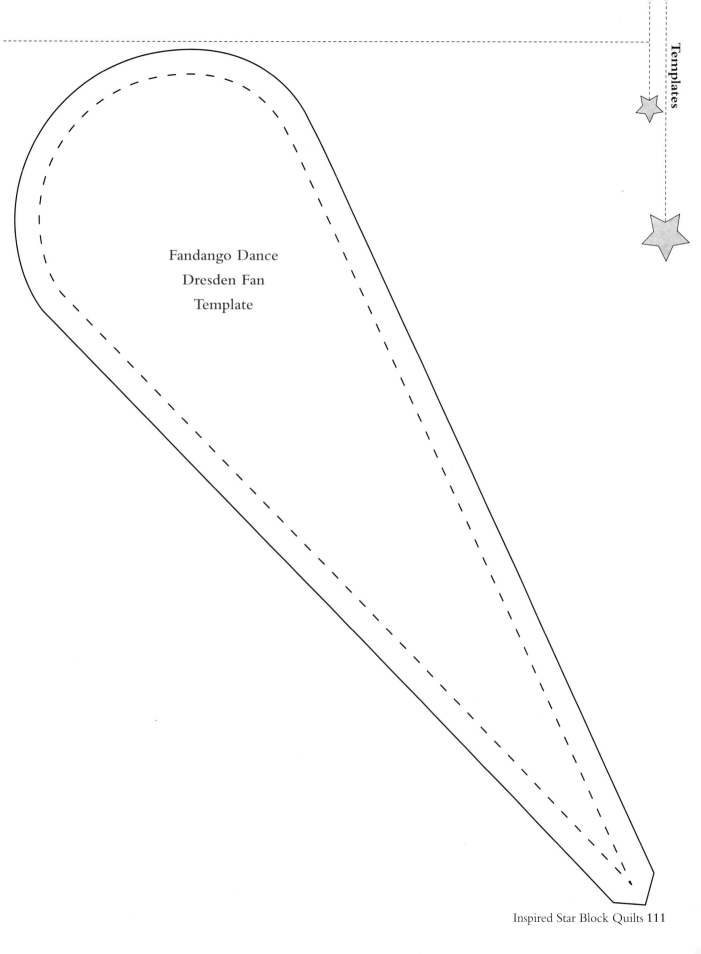

Fandango Dance
Dresden Fan
Template

About the Author

Born in St. Paul, Minnesota, Sandy Berg was raised in the Twin Cities area. Her father was in the Air Force so she has also lived in North Carolina, Kansas, and Japan. As a child and young adult, she was always attracted to various needlework skills. She learned to sew clothing at an early age, knit (thanks to a prolific knitting aunt), crochet, embroider, and many other needlecrafts. When she discovered quilting, it was all over—she was hooked for a lifetime.

She now lives in Lewiston, Idaho, with her husband, Jerry, and two step-children, three grandchildren, and two great granddaughters make up her family. Spreading her quilts among family and friends, in 2009 she began sharing her efforts with military personnel by way of the Quilts Of Valor® Foundation. There will always be weddings, births, birthdays, and other special occasions for which to make quilts, but the Quilts of Valor effort gets many of her quilt projects these days. She enjoys reading, gardening, and cooking when she is not quilting.

In 2010, Sandy launched a quilt pattern company, Raspberry Bramble Designs (*www.raspberrybrambledesigns.com*). She continues to design new patterns and teach locally. Helping new quilters find pleasure in quilt-making brings joy and fulfillment to her life.

Acknowledgments

Some of my QOV friends have been instrumental in the creation of the quilts presented here. My great thanks to Sharon Ledbetter, Alice Gwinn, Kelly McKeehan, Shelley Nagel, Kate Pippen, and Nancy Larson-Powers—you have my deepest gratitude for all the help and encouragement you have given me. I wouldn't want to have done this without you backing me up!

To In The Beginning Fabrics—thank you for Jason Yenter's "Unusual Garden" fabric. It is the perfect setting for the "Providence" quilt. To the wonderful staff at Landauer Publishing—thank you for your faith in me and for all the help and encouragement you have given me. You have helped to make a dream come true!

Dedication

To my loving husband, Jerry, who has always believed in me. Your love means everything to me! To the memory of my parents, Elmer and Jeanie Witham, who were always proud of my accomplishments, big and small. They taught me that anything was possible with dedication and hard work.